Photograph by JERRY MONROE

About the Author

Brent Wade grew up in Anne Arundel County, Maryland,
and graduated from the University of Maryland with a
degree in English. He has worked as a manager for
AT&T, and in marketing and merchandising for both
Westinghouse and LSI Logic. He and his wife live in
Gambrills, Maryland, with their two young sons. He is
at work on a second novel.

"A thought-provoking, compelling look at the life of a black man in corporate America . . . riveting reading. What makes *Company Man* especially fascinating is that its social theme is wrapped in a wonderful, suspenseful, captivating story."

— *Orlando Sentinel*

"A tense, unpredictable story of the irresolvable conflicts blacks face in white-collar America . . . Wade never merely targets the white-collar world. He dissects it, evincing familiar ideas with freshness and suspense."

— *Los Angeles Reader*

"A fictional look at the so-called affirmative action generation that is witty but frightening in its accuracy."

— *Emerge*

"An unforgettable look at white corporate culture from the viewpoint of a keen-eyed observer and one who has spent his share of time being observed — if only for the color of his skin. This is an auspicious debut."

— *New Orleans Times-Picayune*

"Timely and insightful."

— *The Virginian-Pilot* (Norfolk, Va.)

"An astute and provocative examination of an aspect of black life rarely addressed in fiction."

— *Flint Journal*

company man

company man

a novel by

Brent Wade

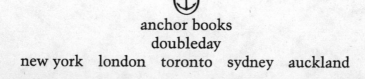

anchor books
doubleday
new york   london   toronto   sydney   auckland

An Anchor Book

PUBLISHED BY DOUBLEDAY

a division of Bantam Doubleday Dell Publishing Group, Inc.
666 Fifth Avenue, New York, New York 10103

Anchor Books, Doubleday, and the portrayal of an anchor are trademarks of
Doubleday, a division of Bantam Doubleday Dell Publishing Group, Inc.

Company Man was originally published in hardcover by Algonquin Books of
Chapel Hill in 1992. The Anchor Books edition is published by arrangement with
Algonquin Books of Chapel Hill.

Design by B. Williams & Associates.

Library of Congress Cataloging-in-Publication Data
Wade, Brent, 1959–
    Company man : a novel / by Brent Wade. — 1st Anchor Books ed.
      p. cm.
    I. Title.
PS3573.A313C6   1993
813'.54 – dc20   92-26961
                                                        CIP

ISBN 0-385-42563-5

Many thanks to Clay Perry, Aimee Doyle, Chip Graber, and the incredible Charles Carroll Mish. A moment of silence, as well, for the late Walter Fisher, without whom this book could not have been written.

For Yvette,
who even through that well-known hour
of supreme darkness held out faith to me
with the certainty of another day.

The truth is, we do not know how to deal with dreams;
what they tell is uncertain and they do not all come true.
For there are two different gates which let out the shadowy
dreams: one is made of horn, one of polished elephant's tooth.
The elephant's tooth is full of untruth, so that any dreams
which come through never come true. But carven horn is
ne'er forsworn and if one had a dream which came by that
gate, it tells him the truth.

— Homer, *Odyssey*

company man

one

Thank you for your letters. Yes, I have been reading them, to answer one of your questions. I'm sorry I've taken so long to reply, but I've been engrossed in a project. Nothing you should know about just yet. I've abandoned it for now anyway. But for the longest time it required every spare moment I could steal.

I actually only got around to your letters this past week. I had kept them bundled together in the top drawer of my night table. But I've read every last one of them now and I hope that in creating this journal I answer all your questions. I notice you ask a lot of things about the past. (What does that have to do with anything now?) I suppose though that first card I sent you was something of a teaser, as you said. A postcard just doesn't have space for much more. I thought if nothing else you would comment on the photo, but you never mentioned it. Postcards depicting the best of Baltimore's "world-famous block" are especially rare in the gift shop at Johns Hopkins Hospital. Donna had to look all over town for that card. She says it's the most realistic photo she's ever seen on a postcard. Why that matters to her I'm not sure.

Have I told you about Donna, Donna Lindo? She's the ward nurse here in the evenings. (She has an ass that could raise the dead!) I don't quite know how to describe her to you. She's what we would have called "spooky" in the old days because of her seriousness and her penchant for speaking in metaphors. Originally, she's from one of the islands—Jamaica, Barbados, Martinique, someplace like that. I'm not sure. But she's been in Baltimore most of her adult life and whatever accent she had is now barely perceptible. You can hear it most noticeably in words containing the letter o. She invariably rolls the sound into another syllable so that it coos. My name, on her tongue, comes out as "Billy Coovingtoon." But even if you didn't notice her speech you would still think she was from someplace else. There's a quality about her—an unstudied aloofness, some hybrid form of self-assurance? You know there's something about her you just don't find in your average American Negro.

These days, Donna is the only one I'll talk to. We, in fact, talk quite a bit to each other. For some reason she doesn't seem to have the problem understanding me that Paula and Dr. Theodore experience. (My speech is so badly slurred now it's almost unrecognizable.) And she doesn't ask me a lot of questions like Paula or that damned Greek with his patronizing seventy-five-dollar-an-hour earnestness. I've stopped answering questions. What's the point? The whole thing's been on the local news, in the local papers—although I've not seen the face of one reporter. There was one, though, a man who claimed to be a writer of some kind. I'm not even sure of his name; they wouldn't let him on the ward. Paula told me later that he had approached her. He said he was a freelance writer working on a story about corporate life and how it affects *us*. She didn't want to talk to him. There wasn't much she could have told him anyway. After a while he stopped trying to call her; then he just dropped out of sight.

But suppose I had been able to talk to him? Suppose Dr. Theodore had let him come onto the ward to speak with me, what then? I would have told him about the grim significance of my discovery. I would have given my version of the events. I would have tried to make him see what happened through my eyes and perhaps make him understand that the nature of self-deception is that it's always what someone else does. I don't think it would have even been newsworthy that way. And even if it generated one byline, what good would it do? What can we really expect to change in these final waning dog days of the twentieth century? The great alabaster consciousness would have prevailed, untouched. So I keep my mouth shut. Like I said, what's the point anymore?

But for completeness' sake, I'll tell you what the papers did say. You deserve nothing less than a balanced account. Donna saved a clipping from *The Sun*. She of course didn't know me then, she had just read the article and found it strangely incomplete. And so she clipped it. I think most people would see an event itself as news and stop there. But Donna knows that the reporting of the news is perhaps the most telling news. I'll copy the gist of the article for you.

Roland Park Man Wounded in Robbery Attempt

A Baltimore man was rushed to Johns Hopkins Shock Trauma Center late yesterday evening with a gunshot wound to the head, the victim in an apparent robbery attempt. The incident occurred in the 5600 block of Roland Avenue, in the heart of Roland Park, one of northern Baltimore's oldest and most fashionable neighborhoods.

Police are withholding the man's name and would not comment on the details of the incident. But *The Sun* has learned that the man, 38-year-old William Covington, had apparently surprised a burglar in his basement and was wounded in the ensuing struggle. Mr. Covington is a longtime Roland Park resident and a high-ranking executive with the Varitech Industries.

Ironically, this incident has occurred during what was already a tense time for Mr. Covington. According to an anonymous source, Covington had recently been placed on administrative leave pending an investigation into charges of alleged sexual harassment. A spokesperson for Varitech declined to comment on the charge.

That's pretty much it. The rest is just filler. I'm curious as to the source of that information about my problems at work—not that I'm denying any of it. It's just that I don't know how anyone outside Varitech would have known about it. And that stuff about surprising a burglar, that had to have come from Paula. She still denies it, but I know how preoccupied she's become with how things will look, and so I remain suspicious of her. She's probably scared For Sale signs up all along the block. But then again, I think the folks in that neighborhood are dug in for the duration.

Would you like to know the simple truth?—not that it's any big secret now. There was no burglar. I fired the shot. I screwed up, though, since all I managed to do was maim myself. I didn't think it would be so difficult. I thought all I had to do was place the muzzle of my thirty-two anywhere on my head and squeeze the trigger. After all, how could anyone pierce his brain and survive? Part of the problem was the service that the neighborhood receives. The paramedics must be block-patroling around there.

Next time I'll give it more thought. But as I told you I've abandoned that project for now. That's why I'm on this ward under observation. That's Donna's real job; she's my emotional sentinel.

I'm afraid I've waited too late to start this journal. I'm getting tired. It's the Demerol Donna gave me earlier. The dosages are very low, but it's overpowering stuff. Paula will be coming by in the morning so I won't have much time. Don't worry, though, I haven't forgotten your questions. I'll try to write a little more tomorrow evening.

two

Did I ramble yesterday? The Demerol sometimes has that effect. It makes me hyper then it makes me listless.

Paula came in today. I guess she's close to seven months along now. Her stomach looks so tight and uncomfortable that I can hardly imagine her getting much larger. I haven't mentioned anything about Paula or the baby, have I? To be honest I've been trying not to think about them. It only reminds me of how awful things are now.

Were you shocked to hear from me after all these years? There was not a hint of it in your letters. You too then must know that there is always an understanding between close friends—some minute infrangible charge that always seems to bond, despite ourselves. I was always certain that I'd hear from you again—not like this, though. I had expected to spot you on a street somewhere, at a bus stop perhaps, picking a rebel speck of lint from your suit. You would reply, calmly (never being one to register surprise), "Hello, Billy," as if all that time in between had been nothing more than an energizing summer nap. But there I go again playing scenarist. It's just a smaller part of this whole sickness of contriving portions of your life. You tend to forget what you've made up. Do it enough and you won't even remember the door you came in through. Am I lapsing into excursiveness again?

You asked about the accommodations here. What can I tell you? One hospital room looks like another. The nurses (with the exception of Donna) are all black girls from West Baltimore with names like Kerisha, Twanda, and Danita. They'll bring in my lunch and say, "Here you lunch, Mista Coventen." They're all as nice as they can be, though, every last one of them, even though I don't do much more than smile at them and throw food on occasion when I'm not left alone. They think I'm crazy anyway.

If I could complain about anything here it would be the view from my window. It faces smack into the south wall of the hospital. The most I ever used to see of the outdoors was the sunlight and shadows falling along the wall. But now that spring has arrived I've been entertained by the comings and goings of a pair of starlings. They're trying to build a nest in the crook of an old rainspout. You were always interested in things like that, wildlife and such, weren't you? In the fall, we'd go rabbit hunting after school and as we walked through the briars you would tell me in your slow deliberate way things like the difference between a rabbit and a hare.

"It's funny," you would say, "that hares are actually born hairless."

I remember saving your ass in a fight once too. You were never much with your fists. Thomas Queen wanted your head because he had concluded that you tried to "act white." What he meant was you spoke correct English, got good grades, and generally tended to associate with the "brains" (most of whom happened to be skinny dweebish white boys) more than was proper for a black person. He had also heard that you had routinely referred to him as a "dumb, gold-toothed street nigger." Thomas outweighed me by thirty pounds and ended up kicking my ass royally. It never affected our friendship, though; we had found a community with each other when we were very young. We were both fatherless. Mine had died in a fire; yours took off before you were born.

Lately, a lot of things have been coming back to me about you. Details in bits and pieces. Last night, before I dozed off, I remembered that you had a nickname. Isn't it odd that should come back? It just struck me all of a sudden that you were once called something else. Pee Wee, Pee Wee Walker. I started the whole thing in the seventh grade. You were so short no one thought you would grow. But you got in all of your growing at once and by high school you were the tallest among us. Then we called you Zip, because you made it to the state track meet every year in the 220. Zip never stuck like Pee Wee. Did we really speak that genteelly of one another? Pee Wee, Zip, today you'd be "that little mafucker," perhaps "fuckin' fast Walker."

I also remember how bright you were and the odd way— the only way—some of our teachers accepted that. Mrs. Cables, Mrs. Lucy Cables from French II ("I didn't know we had any colored boys in Roberts as smart as you; makes me wonder how unequal our education system ever really was"). I recall other times. After that last track meet at Annapolis; you and I sitting in the locker room in our drawers, me helping you rewrite a speech you were to give on Awards Day. That was June 1965, do you recall? You were class valedictorian, "the first Negro to attain such an honor at Roberts Senior High," it was printed in the *Roberts Gazette*.

Of course, we were all news that year. The first Negroes

to graduate from a formerly all-white school, the first fruits of integration. Back then I wanted to be a novelist— having no real idea of what that want demanded, but convincing myself that it seemed an appropriately lofty goal to authenticate my "new Negro" status. Of course you always knew you wanted to be an archaeologist. I remember listening to you explain to your mother exactly what that was. I don't know if she ever saw much merit in digging up old things, but she was proud of you; we all were. What giant steps we were expected to take in those days. And I suppose you did, but me, I was never book-smart like you. I tended to rely more on my deftness, my presence at the aesthetic moment. I did have talent, but yours was much greater. We felt it took precedence over any aptitudes the rest of us might have had, a racial altruism. You were the one who deserved the limelight that last year of high school and we wanted you to have all of it. Actually, for me it was all a bit more selfish than altruistic. I knew I could slip-stream in your brilliance. For you were front-page stuff: athlete, scholarship recipient, first in your class. You had the folks at Stanford waiting for you with open arms. A few of the local TV news crews made Awards Day that year and there was even wild talk that Walter Cronkite would broadcast the story.

Were you a homosexual even then or was it something that developed later during the summer before your first year of college? I've never had the guts to ask you until now or, for that matter, ask you just what it is to be that way. I've heard different things. Is it a way of thinking, or something else? I read an article several years ago in *Time* or *Newsweek*, somewhere, that said homosexual men have as many as one hundred different lovers a year. Of course that was before AIDS, but was it true? It's an impressive number if it's correct. Frankly, it's hard for me to believe. I don't think I've made love to more than four different women in my entire life. But if you tell me the numbers are what swayed you, Paul, I'd almost be able to understand. There's some notion of cause and effect in that. As it stands, though, I'm at a loss to know why you went the way you did. There's so much I've never understood about it.

I can't even bring myself to use the word "gay." There's a casualness about it that's too awkward and unearned for me. And there are questions, a lot of questions I've wanted to ask you for a long time. There are things I've wanted you to explain to me. Over the years, I've searched for an explanation of my own, attempting to link cause and effect, action and reaction. Nothing seems to fit. I get dizzy thinking of how jumbled things have become. How could the closest of friends lose contact with each other for nineteen years? Everything has happened so unexplainably ass-backward.

It should have been that around the time I married Paula you would also have taken a wife. We'd live a couple of doors apart from each other, have fabulous jobs in some fabulous city, and have dinner together twice a week. During dessert, while Paula and your missus served up the peach cobbler, you and I could bore them senseless with stories of how we'd catch white perch in Furnace Creek every fall and sometimes take a swim during the few warm Indian summer evenings that remained. We'd hang our clothes over the sumac and wade out until the bottom got too muddy. Remember the sumac in the fall? The leaves got redder than match tips. (Do you have sumac in Palo Alto? They say California has everything.) Maybe over a bourbon and water you would even bashfully tell us about the time you screwed Crystal Merritt in her mother's bed. When I think of that now all I can do is wonder how you could screw Crystal three times in an afternoon and still ask me to hold you. Wasn't it enough that I loved you like a brother?

When word got around about you in Roberts, it fractured just about everyone. But then I don't think many people in southern Maryland are as shatterproof as you seem to be. Your mother wasn't. She even gave up churchgoing for a time (although I'm sure she prays for you still) and eventually left Roberts for good. Retreating back to her people, to her birth state of Alabama, as if that land were a crawlspace to cool and shield her from the heat and glare of a high-noon sun.

Something else I've wanted to ask you for some time now: why did you write those letters to everyone, announcing it, for God's sake, as if it were a wedding? Was it some grand way to get back at me for rejecting you after you had confided in me, or were you just making sure there wouldn't be a way back home? You had the collective pride of five hundred or so countrified descendants of slaves looking to you as if you were a promise from God. Those letters you sent were read deeper than you imagine.

My grandmother called it niggerish. Her word for anything that, as she saw it, "sits back collid folks." I'm sure that by now I would represent quite a setback for her. If she were alive today, she would stroll in here, hug me, kiss me, and say, "Boy, what niggerish mess you in now?" It was a word of her generation (although my actions are haunted still by her definitions), a legacy from our self-hating, keep-grinning, shoe-shuffling, make-no-waves past. It was the context of all the judgments she made upon me. Me, the orphaned grandchild whom she would adamantly raise to be "ah edjacated man." If I was dancing to the radio, singing along with a record, or laughing loudly—anything that might draw attention—my grandmother called it niggerish. The year we were told that we would begin junior high in an integrated school, she unabashedly began to push me to emulate white speech (not understanding that it was generally as incorrect as ours but that the real significance was that their mistakes were theirs), white behavior, and to keep in my own space. I don't know what demons drove her. That is perhaps the one gaping incompleteness in what I have to tell you. I am only certain that she loved me and that she had come to see blackness as that mildew that slowly devours the paint on fine picket fences. She would on occasion tell me things like: "You can't depend on collid people; they ain't neva had nothin' cause they come from nothin' and they stingy wit what they do git. A lot of them git a chance and don't do nothin' but mess it up. It's best to stay away from triflin' Nigroes. White folks don't neva put no count in triflin' Nigroes."

I've come to believe now that what she dreamt for was my metamorphosis into a Generic, a man devoid of any cultural affiliation, of any nuance that pointed to obligations and ties that might be seen as different. Different was always pejorative to her. Disassociating ourselves from the semblance of a culture we had garnered and pieced together for ourselves was in her eyes our price, our dowry for the privilege of mingling unfettered among the huddled masses. What she couldn't appreciate was that for *us* Ellis Island is little more than an allusion; Plymouth Rock, an allegory whose significance hovers above the border of irrelevance and myth. And what I didn't understand about the whites I encountered was that *they* held similar sentiments about the industry of chattel and the auction blocks of colonial America. Perhaps this is where it really begins.

I remember my grandmother seeing James Brown on

"The Ed Sullivan Show" for the first time and commenting, "Now don't that look right niggerish." Little Richard was worse than niggerish. And you; well I've already told you where you stood with her after those letters were sent. Although she'd had problems with you since the time you were about eight.

But I should move on. What's to be gained by shadowboxing with the past? These digressions don't answer your questions, I know. I'll try to be more careful. You had asked about my job.

"Building the Future's Foundation, Today," that was the corporate slogan that took us through the seventies. It's not stellar, I'll admit. But it was my idea. At the time, we were paying large sums to Neville, Schwab & Strumm, our Manhattan ad agency, to devise a new corporate logo and slogan. Nothing they had submitted was well received and so I took my idea to our company president, John Haviland. Actually, he wasn't president then, but a very powerful general manager in our government-products division. I didn't actually "take" my idea to him either. I was a speechwriter at that time and had gone in to see him about a presentation I was putting together for his talk to the board of directors. In the midst of our meeting he made a comment about the ad agency's inability to come up with a meaningful slogan. That's when I put forward my idea, more as a joke really since it was similar to something I'd heard the night before on television. But Haviland liked it. He liked it so much he put his weight behind its adoption.

Suggesting that slogan was really the beginning of my career at Varitech because through that one act I gained John Haviland's patronage. He began first to speak to me when we passed each other in the cafeteria, occasionally pointing me out to his colleagues as "the guy behind our new motto." Sometimes he would stop me in the hall and invite me to talk about whatever new projects I happened to be working on. You must understand the nature of patronage; it's something of a Möbius strip on which power and security twist and orbit as one perpetually complementary force. You see, what the patron requires most from the recipient is loyalty. The more loyalty displayed, the more opportunity the patron will bestow, since this loyalty, however mercenary, is the only real external security the patron can have against the atavism of corporate life. The recipient, aware of his role in this symbiosis, responds in turn, feeding the patron an even greater sense of power and security and so on, ad infinitum. Of course, the more power the patron grants, the greater the loyalty demanded. It's the foundation of the old boy system. To understand this is to understand why the top jobs at Varitech (and probably a lot of American companies) seem historically peopled by men strikingly similar to one another. Executives are most likely to trust what they're familiar with.

John Haviland's overtures were therefore of historical proportion. But this was an aspect of the times. I'm certain his intention was to be a groundbreaker—the first executive to have a black on his staff. It was important for him to appear contemporary without seeming to threaten the infrastructure. He also knew that my loyalty was perhaps more assured than most, since his offer was the only one I was likely to receive. He knew I would have no real options. It was in many ways a shrewd move. But then that was expected; Haviland was after all a young lion, a man slated to be going places in the corporation. When he offered me a position in his organization as his executive assistant I accepted instantly. He told me that he had bigger things in mind for me but that he would have to move slowly. Even if

I hadn't believed him, what was there to lose? Within a year I was promoted; I began to work more closely with Haviland and through him other executives. By that route, I was regularly promoted right up to the year Fred Boland retired and I took his job. My business card now reads William Covington, Director of Marketing Communications, Varitech Industries, Inc.

I wasn't smack in the middle of executive row, but I had a big office adjoined by a slightly smaller room that housed my two subordinates and my secretary. I even had the defrocked sales manager from the company's military-products group in the office across the hall. Lloyd Harrow was the youngest son of one of the company's major stockholders. A good family with a good part of downtown Philadelphia in their name. Honest to God blue blood. That was about the only explanation one could give of Lloyd's existence—a senior sales manager at twenty-eight, with no technical background and no wife. We became friends (he had heard that I owned a Jaguar; he had three, loved the cars, loved to talk about them). I remember how very impressive it all seemed. This was real wealth, two steps down the hall. And although I didn't know what he had done to become John Haviland's special projects manager—an appellation that signified his lack of a meaningful job—I couldn't help feeling that his presence on the hall lent a certain credibility to me.

I sometimes felt my job needed legitimizing. By this time my association with Haviland was more legend than day-to-day actuality. He had moved into echelons of power that I could only glimpse. I heard him allude to it once, the day I bought the Jag. I was driving him to a dinner we were both attending and when I asked him how things were going he looked over to me with a half smile and said,

"Well, if you should only talk about what you know and work's all you talk about, then something's wrong."

What I was more known for now, what my department did, was coordinate the production of ads, brochures, trade shows, and other promotional activities. Wrapping all things in their best light. If Varitech were a company that produced package goods—soft drinks, any consumer item— my function would perhaps have been much more crucial. As it was, we produced very specialized machinery for the electronics industry, and in a company of mechanical and electrical engineers, marketing communications was looked upon largely as a helpful but not entirely necessary part of the business. Most held the politely reticent opinion that what sold our products wasn't the slick advertising, or slicker brochures, or anything else we did, but rather the pricing structures, availability, and technical sophistication of our products. What I really did (to their thinking) was image promotion. Varitech as leader; Varitech as formidable institution; Varitech as corporate hydra with nine heads raging in eight different markets.

Then too there was the fact that funding for my group came directly out of company profits. Not only was our role in the sale of our products debatable (who can say for certain at what level a person or group is first persuaded?), but we were also an overhead expense. There was always grumbling about wasted money and doing away with the department. But that's unlikely to happen. In addition to Haviland's strong support, there's just too much paranoia about what the lack of image promotion might reveal. Of course in the end, that could be the diagnosis of my own troubles.

But let me not draw so disparaging a picture. There was a lot of upside. The world of business could be invigorating in its excitement and frenetic pace. And while my role at the boardroom meetings and long-term market-planning sessions may have been diaphanous (if not invisible), all in all it was a pleasant, comfortable rut. There was a certain coital snugness about it. I had a great salary, the patronage of the company president, a beautiful wife, a handsome old house, and a cardinal red XJ6.

three

We were talking about work. Didn't you ask something in one of your letters about my wife's place in all of this? Or did you say simply, "Tell me about your wife"? No matter, both questions are essentially the same since my wife's part in my job is inseparable from my wife. Having a beautiful wife is an asset in the corporate world. For the rising young executives, it's quietly looked upon as one of the rewards of good cocksmanship. There's an attendant prestige for the man with a beautiful wife. Her beauty gets extrapolated somehow into a presumption of his good salesmanship, good marketing skills, or some larger savvy. I suppose this would be true anywhere image is a large and tacit part of one's job description. Perhaps there's some primal root to it all. Who can ever know for sure? What I am certain of is that the wife gets reduced to an accoutrement. That's more than some of the younger wives can take. I've seen them numbed into a kind of bemused reticence at corporate functions.

But Paula played her role with abandon—so well in fact that I'm not really sure when it stopped being an act. Ah, but here again we observe the trick of artifice. I'm speaking again of our tendency to take on a role and then wake up one morning to find that the role has taken us over. You lose track of what came first. Case in point: Paula never shrank from her role as beautiful corporate wife. It was a new part, that of the black corporate wife, so there was a kind of opening-night anticipation from the audience. Perhaps that partially explains the strength of Paula's performance, because Lord was she good at it. I was in tow, struck by her confidence, her odd grace and well-to-do southern black woman's sense of pragmatism. In fourteen years of marriage, I've never seen her bend down from the waist. A small thing I know, but it makes her movements to retrieve anything from the floor take the form of a curtsey. There's a way she says things too: "Hot tea tastes better out of a thin-lipped cup" or "Only homely spinster women wear white shoes for formal dress." There was a logic in all that, inaccessible to me but so stark and clear and dead-center true in the way it made her work that I fell in love first with her bearing, her presence, and then with her. She would bring this same peculiar poise to the role of the engaging corporate wife.

She would accompany me to select executive dinners and marketing Christmas parties and upon entering the room become the absolute center of attention. Granted, at that time we were almost always the only blacks to be seen at these things and so we were noticed. But Paula had her own way of drawing people, a finesse cloaked from me by familiarity. It could be surprising to witness. Most often the show would begin when we were separated, once I had been pulled aside for a quick discussion of a new project or an introduction to a colleague from another department. I would hear Paula's voice over the crowd, those slow, stretched Virginia vowels, followed by a roll of laughter. I would turn to see her surrounded by a group of executive wives. Soon, we husbands would drift over and gradually become part of the same laughter and garrulousness. We would be a team then, Paula and I, working the crowd with a little Lucy and Ricky routine. There would always be compliments afterward: "You've got quite a wife there, Bill" or "I think you're onto something with that wife of yours, young man." I remember feeling that her new status seemed somehow to fill me out like a final detail, like a dream I'd forgotten and suddenly recalled into being. (Could it have been my grandmother's ghost whispering approval?) For the first time in my life, I felt like a part of something larger than where I'd come from, as if having Paula brought a new, more finished texture to my bearing. It was as if through Varitech our union had been consummated, as if Paula and I were now bound by something more expansive than a legal document and two yellow rings.

At times I would almost forget that she was the same woman I'd met in college. The doctor's daughter from Richmond in my major British writers course, who every day would take a seat two places to the right of mine, who seemed to enjoy Dickens as much as I did, and who on the day of our first exam spoke to me for the first time (a very bold move for a woman in '66).

"Excuse me, but don't you run track for Maryland? Aren't you the sprinter who was in the *Diamondback* yesterday?"

I told her I was, that I had indeed come close to breaking a school record in the 100. She smiled and settled back into her seat.

"I was wondering just how long it would take you to say hello to me," she said.

She had her own car, a Windex blue Mustang soft-top,

and she lived off-campus in a little house in east College Park. We drove back there for lunch after the exam.

"I couldn't stand living on-campus," she told me. "There was only one other black girl on my hall and she was so nervous and scared. White colleges intimidate a lot of us who grew up segregated. Poor Eva; she'd even shower after everyone was asleep. But she was someone to talk to. When she transferred to Howard last semester I decided to move. Otherwise"—she said this with a dramatic weariness, full of aplomb—"it would have been just me and all those simple white girls. No one was outright hostile, but I got so tired of them asking me what I was doing every time I had a straightening comb in my hand."

"Your parents let you live alone?" I asked.

"I live with my Aunt Edna, but she's not home until after nine tonight."

The lunch she had promised was not the tuna sandwich I'd envisioned. She fried two generous pork chops and warmed over a pot of collards.

"Won't your aunt miss this?" I asked.

"The pork chops are mine," she said. "Aunt Edna doesn't even eat pork. She says it's slave food." She had her back to me, speaking out from the tiny kitchen above the cackle and sputter of the frying meat. "We buy our groceries separately, and Aunt Edna always cooks more collards than she can eat. They would have just gone to waste."

When everything was ready, she put the food on a green plastic plate and set it down in front of me.

"Aren't you going to eat anything?" I said, looking at her now through the rising steam. "Or do you think it's slave food too?" I wanted to see if she knew the truth, that no slave would have eaten from this part of the pig. I was trying to assign a level of awareness to her demeanor. She was unlike any black woman I had ever met. She had the same capacity for nonchalance, the same informal sense of self-assurance that I had only seen before in very attractive white women. I wanted to know more about her. It wasn't even a sexual curiosity; I wanted to know what lay behind the anomaly. As I mentioned earlier, I was in tow.

"No, I don't think it's slave food, not a chop, anyway," she said, casually. "I'd rather just watch you eat. You can tell a lot about a person by the way he eats."

We talked away the afternoon, skipping our other classes that day. She was also an English major and thought it understandable that more blacks didn't opt for that curriculum. "There's not a lot of money to be made with a B.A. in English," she said. The impact of that statement might be lost today, since I understand a lot of college kids are very career (read "money") oriented. But back then, colleges for the most part had not yet become the trade schools they are today. Her statement seemed truly odd. It turned me defensive. I felt compelled to tell her of my goal to become a writer. "Really? That's pretty ambitious," she replied. "A lot of people think they can write books. Have you read *The Fire Next Time*?"

At the end of the year, when I met her parents for the first time, she would tell me not to mention anything about wanting to be a writer to her father. "Tell him you want to be a journalist. He'll be more impressed with something that sounds like a real profession."

Not that the gainfulness of my intended livelihood would have made much difference to her mother—a honey-colored woman with a bronze tint in her hair and the lease on her daughter's green eyes. No, Naomi Bond would find me more than suitable, novelist and all, if for no other reason than that her daughter wished it so. But Paula had

talked so much about her father that I had almost anticipated her concern over how my ambitions would be presented to him. On our first lunch date, and countless times
thereafter, Paula spoke about her father with an almost
biblical reverence. I learned that for a time he had been the
most prominent physician in black Richmond—a circumstance that had made him respected and wealthy in that
community. (Many of the monied local whites knew of him
as well.) He ran the local NAACP chapter and had worked a
few years earlier to register voters and stage one or two of
the sit-ins in downtown Richmond diners. According to
Paula, he had even received a congratulatory letter from Dr.
King. As the decade grew more tumultuous her father had
become so well known in Richmond that for a while whenever whites and blacks got together to talk in small official
numbers, Nathaniel Bond could always be found in the eye
of the storm.

It might have been argued that even some of the local
ministers weren't held in as high regard as Nathaniel Bond.
To his section of Richmond he was as true a prophecy, as
much a witness to the justness, power, and promise of
believing as the blustery reiterations of any minister.

Here was a man who had grown up poor in the capital of
the Old South. At a time when parades were held for
Confederate war dead, when the black man's place was one
of unquestioned servitude and inferiority, when the sanc-
tity of the culture demanded that the slightest public expression of dignity or disapproval be met with crushing
brutality. Somehow Nathaniel Bond had flourished in that
environment. He had managed to find a niche that escaped
scrutiny, and he had indeed endured and very obviously
prospered. (The Bond home remains a testament to the neo-
affluent grandeur aesthetic. You know, Waterford salt

shakers and all.) There were always a few like him, men who beat the odds. Ironically, these men would be used by southern segregationists and their soul mates as examples of the separate but equal opportunity that existed under Jim Crow.

"It's some bizarre form of denial. They minimize and legitimize," Dr. Bond was fond of saying.

I became well acquainted with the term during my first visit, for he used it often that evening. We had a long, almost lurid conversation about the South and the civil-rights movement and the young Turks he felt were destroying it. This was near the end of 1966, a year that had seen rioting in New York and Chicago and other northern cities.

The precariousness of that time became an extension of Dr. Bond's own experiences: He talked vigorously about his life, his struggle. He emphasized that there was a "right way" to go about things. I did a good deal of listening that evening.

He told me that the most galling indignity of his boyhood had been the knowledge that even the most ignorant, shiftless white man knew he was your better.

"That Colored Only sign didn't say college graduates exempted," he reminded me.

I guess you could say we got along wonderfully, despite the fact that I hadn't had an opportunity to say much. Paula's admonitions were beginning to seem overstated (although journalism had turned out to be a fine profession in her father's eyes).

A little later into the evening, as the women cleared the dinner table, Dr. Bond showed me his library. I understood instinctively that he had allowed me entrance to someplace private—a region of himself as vital and as incontestably real to him as the huge cream-colored door he opened before me. The room was immense, perhaps as large as the entire downstairs of my grandmother's house. The walls were covered with books, neatly ranked on heavy oak shelves. I had never considered that a black man might possess such a thing as a private library. It was an impressive sight. But what he told me next was even more astounding. The entire library had been constructed around a single theme: the repudiation of that substrative belief that the black man had not contributed anything useful to mankind. His library was a kind of personal substantiation.

"They don't want to acknowledge it," he told me, "but the truth is the modern world got its start from Africans—not the Greeks like they would have you believe, but Africans." He showed me some books on early Egyptian culture, photos of wall paintings and statues of dark-skinned Cushite Pharaohs of Nubia mentioned, he told me, in the Bible in the Second Book of Kings as the protector of the Israelites. He showed me books on excavated cities from the interior of Africa, the walls of Great Zimbabwe, and other places from the upper and lower Nile with names like Meroë and Axum. Some displayed architectural features found on Greek buildings constructed much later, he explained. He showed references by ancient Greek authors to the majesty of African civilization and the ingenuity of her people. Some of the passages he read aloud and it seemed that by simply saying the words he was freed somehow.

"Herodotus, from Halicarnassus in 430 B.C., says what was generally known to be true then. He says, 'There is much gold to be found in Ethiopia.... The men too are the tallest, the best-looking, and the longest-lived people in the world.'" He looked at me as if expecting some statement of agreement. But I had nothing to say. What did I know of the ancient world? Anyway, the look must have been rhetorical because he continued as if I didn't matter.

"Listen to this," he said, opening another book. "This is from a Sicilian historian from 50 B.C., Diodorus. He says, 'The Ethiopians were the first of all men, and the proof of this historians agree are manifest.' "

I thought I should try to say something intelligent this time. So I said, "Wow, that's heavy stuff. I—"

"That's right, and over here they try to tell us we look like monkeys and that the colored man has never been nothin'—but listen, listen to the rest of it. He says that the Egyptians are colonists sent out by the Ethiopians and that most Egyptian customs are Ethiopian. We're a great people, Billy. We are."

I could do nothing but nod my head. It was clear that any verbal response was really unnecessary. I had become a congregation of one.

"And you know what else?" he said. "The Bible wasn't written in Europe! It's just something else they took over and made their own. They're the world's most parasitic people." He would have shown me every book in the library had I let him. But I made a very polite remark about the long tiring drive Paula and I had made from Maryland. And he nodded, as if he realized he needed to regain himself. He would not mention the library to me again for a long time. But I had seen a part of him that I don't think many people had.

To say that he simply had pride would not go far enough toward an explanation. There was something much more intangible at the heart of it—although I was blind to it at the time. I came away with a lasting impression of some other clandestine hunger. The house, the stories of hardship and success, the need for a particular level of respect, the political clout, his library of orphaned history—it was all a testament to cultural estrangement. His wealth had given him the opportunity to explore what for most of us is an unarticulated musing, the anomie of a stranded people. But having faced it, he disguised it as some new cosmology he was trying to create. Another affectation of a man with money. It was the way he sublimated his anger; I understand that now. His library was a universe of possibility, a universe where legitimacy and full-scale acceptance could exist for him unconditionally. It was even deserved. In the mandala of Nathaniel Bond, Jesus was not the blue-eyed sandy-haired Son of God of the white Christian world. He was a dark-eyed Jew from North Africa, broad nosed, thick lipped, as brown as old sandalwood.

"More like us than them," he had said, and I didn't understand then why he needed to believe it.

Some things are clearer to me today. Nathaniel Bond suffered from the disease of the deferred. So he had given himself histories. One of these was a history of his life in Richmond, which he embellished with Dickensian detail. The other history was the one of his people and it stretched back further than the written word would allow. It was all an attempt to put distance between what he was trying to be and what he knew he still was. As if every dollar he made, every speech he gave, every committee he chaired, every trip into his library took him further and further from where he began, from where he was, from where he had never really strayed.

His daughter was of a similar mind, having been nurtured in the humus of her father's reputation. Unlike him, though, she didn't have much to seek restitution from. His lead gray memories (which could never be hers) stood in blind substitution to her own true desire to duplicate what she had known all of her life. She had grown up comfortable and happy, the only child of an important man. She had been insulated from the harsher realities of segregated Richmond. Her run-ins had been minor. She had gone to private schools in New England. She'd spent many summers traveling abroad. No insecurities for Paula Bond; she had grown up a secure fixture in a prominent family who moved within the stratum of black Richmond like a sepia imitation of old Dixie gentility. What she inherited from her father was the expectation that her life should be filled with nothing but nice things and comfort.

Three years after I met her parents for the first time, Paula and I announced our engagement. I had just been hired by Varitech on a tip from a university guidance counselor who had told me, "That's a good place to apply now; a few years back, forget it. But for minorities the door is wide open now."

Paula was obligated to do things properly, "for Momma and Daddy's sake," she assured me. So we made a trip to Richmond so I could formally ask Nathaniel Bond for his daughter's hand in marriage. We made the trip on a Friday evening right after work, taking the new Dodge Dart I'd financed through the Varitech credit union. Paula was working at a bank in Washington then, still living with her spinster Aunt Edna—a woman I remember only as tall, bug-eyed, and quiet. She never spoke more than two words to me the entire time I knew her.

Things in Richmond went well. I came away with Dr. Bond's blessings and a promise for a down payment on a home. That was 1969, two days before Christmas Eve. Paula and I were married the following fall in one of the largest weddings black Richmond had seen in quite some time.

Soon afterward we settled into northern Baltimore, right around the time a lot of whites were fleeing to the suburbs. The '68 riot still had a lot of people skittish. We were the first blacks to live in the neighborhood. We bought our home from an elderly couple who thought that Realtors' commissions were excessive and so had put the house on the market themselves. We got a good deal. A seven-room Tudor with all the amenities of a home built in the late thirties—oak floors, two fireplaces, even a back porch with a swing. And our neighbors? They have been nothing if not kind. We've only heard one remotely disparaging remark. Actually Paula overheard it at the bus stop. Two old Roland Park ladies were discussing which of the new bus routes provided the most direct downtown access. They hadn't noticed Paula when one of them remarked: "Oh, but I don't think any of *us* ride the eighty-nine."

Hardly a brick through the front window. I think Paula and I laughed about it in fact. The times were that good. A week before we closed on the house, Paula found a new job as the admissions director at Morgan State University, a small black school not far from the house. She still works there.

Everything changed after our third year of marriage. Not a change for the worse necessarily, just the normal settling limitations of what's possible. It's the companion of growing older. You have to live with knowing that some things aren't going to happen. Of course the hardest part of that is the realization itself. In our case it began when people started to wonder aloud about just when Paula and I would begin a family. Mrs. Bond would say, "You mean to tell me that great big house for just two people?" It was understandable that the Bonds were anxious to have grandchildren, with Paula being their only child. The fact was she had stopped taking the pill almost a year earlier. Her doctor had told her not to expect any quick results, but to give it at least a year.

So every month, for the next twelve months, Paula counted down the days following her period. She'd take her temperature to determine the exact time of ovulation and we'd have sex on cue. Then there would be the suspense of waiting to see if her period would begin again. We followed that pattern for a year, like experimenting scientists. I began to mark the passage of time by her menstrual cycle. In the spring of the following year we changed doctors. My sperm was tested and Paula was reexamined. That's when we discovered that Paula would probably never have children. She had a condition her doctor called endometriosis, which meant that she had developed scarring in her fallopian tubes. He put her chances at conceiving at less than 15 percent. There was nothing to be done about it.

Paula was devastated. I think for the first time in her life she had been denied something she wanted. For three months she was unable to sleep. She sat up, pillow against the headboard, staring out the window across the rooftops, weeping intermittently. "What do you do when you've thought of yourself in a certain way your whole life, and then you find out you were wrong?" she asked me one night. That was rare; usually there was no conversation. Nothing I could say would comfort her. (What could I know to say at twenty-five anyway?) Her only comfort seemed to be in the most basic of physical acts. A hug, a kiss, the presence of ourselves confining ourselves. We would sacrifice speech completely at these times, preferring only to exchange those feelings one is aware of without the necessity of language, like anguish in a child's face.

She refused to say anything to her father about what had

happened. I've never completely understood why. But when she told her mother, she swore her to secrecy. Mrs. Bond took a train up from Richmond the following week (she's always been afraid to fly). I don't know what she told her husband; I don't know how he couldn't have known what was happening. She stayed with us for a week, spending a lot of quiet time with Paula. The three of us had dinner at Café des Artistes the night before she left. Nothing seemed to have changed. Mrs. Bond's presence hadn't had much effect on Paula's disposition. We were all beginning to worry. Once or twice I brought up the subject of counseling. Her mother called and suggested a similar course of action.

Another month passed. Then one Saturday morning she woke me early and said, "Let's take a ride to Towson this morning." She almost seemed her old self. But I treated it cautiously. I didn't question her until we'd veered off Northern Parkway onto York Road.

"Can I ask why we're going to Towson now?" I said.

"Of course you can," she smiled. "We're going to buy a car."

The car she had in mind was a marshmallow white Mercedes sedan. She paid for it out of a fund her father had set aside for her a few months before our marriage, "just in case things didn't work out between us," she told me as we bickered quietly around the showroom.

We drove it off the lot that same day. I didn't know what to make of it. I wanted to believe that she was okay, but a part of me would not let go of the notion that this was all a harbinger of something terrible. When we got back to the house our neighbors, Bruce and Steffie Waring, walked over to get a closer look at the new car. Bruce, who was a mechanical engineer at Westinghouse, was most interested in the engine. He began a discourse on the virtues of

German engineering that eventually encompassed everything from beer to V-2 rockets. Steffie could not have cared less about that. She was savoring the interior with Paula, running her fingers along the upholstery and dash. We discovered that the Warings too had been interested in a Benz, the same model in fact (although they wanted something in a Bordeaux red).

Paula suggested a ride. That somehow eased my discomfort. It was a healthy, fun idea. We enjoyed Bruce and Steffie. They were the closest things we had to friends in Roland Park. The day we moved into the house they came over and introduced themselves. They were the only couple on the block close to our age. Besides that, they gave great parties and had a lively multiracial group of friends. Only on a few rare occasions did we feel they were going out of their way to prove their hipness, as it was. Bruce made an exaggerated point one evening of letting us know how much he liked what he called "soul food." He used the term with an unabashedness that was meant to suggest some deep and shared understanding between us. He went on to say how he and Steffie would sometimes drive all the way down to Anne Arundel County just for "ribs and greens" at Bill Dotson's. Steffie loved Sly and the Family Stone and Bruce truly thought that James Brown was the greatest one-man show since Moses. (Bruce is still the only white person I've ever heard sing "I Got You" while painting his porch.) Years later, when his first son was born, he named him James— "in tribute to one of my favorite performers," he told us. It was all innocent and flattering, but it made me defensive for reasons I couldn't logically explain.

We took turns driving, the four of us, following a course that took us along the perimeter of the neighborhood. Paula and I had been living there for three years at that time, but riding as a passenger that day it was as if I were seeing the surroundings for the first time. Making our way along Roland Avenue, I saw the almost noble intransigence of those huge muscular old homes. A near self-conscious demeanor in brick and flagstone faces, like any well-preserved antique. A pleasant drowsy elm-lined lithograph.

There was another development that day. It happened after we'd finished our ride and the clamor over the car had dwindled. The Warings soon excused themselves and Paula proceeded to lead me back into the house and upstairs to our bedroom where we made love for the rest of the day. Now a sexually aggressive woman is every man's fantasy. Paula rarely was (usually she had to be drunk). But even that changed.

A lot of things changed in the seventies. I completely abandoned any notion of becoming a novelist. I had stuck to it for a few years, staying up late on weeknights, hovering over my IBM Selectric. But all Paula had to do was stroll by my desk in her nightgown and all I could concentrate on was getting my hands around her bare ass. ("A right nigger-ish disgrace," my grandmother would have said.) This is something I could only admit to an old friend. There was more to it. My responsibilities at Varitech were increasing. I had suddenly become very popular through my association with Haviland. As he gained more power so did I. Over the next few years I would become extremely well known at the company. And Paula would take a kind of stewardship over my career, advising me on what moves to make to keep my standing solidified. The new Jaguar was her idea. She had traded up to another Benz a few years back, but I was still driving around in my Dart. When I was promoted to my current position she took a hard stand.

"You need a new car to go along with the new job," she

insisted one evening, with a kind of shadow seriousness. I wasn't sure how much of it she really meant. We were in the TV room watching a "M*A*S*H" rerun. "An executive should be driving something nicer, especially a black executive. You have to do more to look the part."

So I bought the Jag. I figured I could do worse than wind myself tightly into the fabric of the corporate vestment. I had already adopted the ritual language, the lexicon of shifting responsibility, of keeping myself safe. A lexicon of strategic silences, whispered reassurances, of innuendo and pleasant puppet smiles. It was like learning any new language; when you can dream in it, you're fluent.

four

Donna has just finished bathing me. It would have been impossible without her since the left side of my body is just about useless. My leg is so weak I'm forced to hobble around with a cane. I don't mind the baths at all though. Donna doesn't seem to mind either. I have told you about her haven't I? She and I talk a great deal and she's the most genuinely beautiful woman I've ever seen—in a way distinct from and impossible to compare with Paula. Donna's isn't a fashionable beauty. It's more a suggestion of some vestigial pristineness. There's a grace and assuredness in the way her face comes together—sharp featured and as dark as a strong cup of coffee. A look that suggests bright muslin scarves and scarab bracelets. She has a figure that other women scan discreetly and men stare at with the most niggerish lust imaginable. I've even seen Dr. Theodore steal a glance. Yes, even that stoic old Greek, Dr. Theodore P. Traendofilos, couldn't resist the symmetry of a female behind. I don't know why I should find that surprising though; being a doctor doesn't make him asexual.

You would probably like Dr. Theodore. He has your love of detail. Professionally speaking, there's not really a lot of difference between you two. What does an archaeologist do but study a past in an attempt to reassemble it, to gain an understanding of a way of thinking, a situation in time? As part of both of your professions there's the critical need to make a judgment; you both ultimately play arbiter to some inarticulate broken piece of bone or pottery or flesh.

But this is another digression, isn't it? And I haven't really answered your big question, the one you ask in all of your letters. You want to know why I'm here. You want to know what happened. I'm not entirely sure myself. I remember the events and I've already mentioned my wound. But then I guess that's more of a how than a why. I'll try to get to the heart of it now.

Sometime last year I began having problems maintaining my erections. Actually, it's impossible to give a more precise date because looking back now, it seems to have been a problem for a much longer time. Who would have thought it? Aren't such problems supposedly unknown to us? It's like sunburn; it's not supposed to happen to us, right? I'm only being partially facetious. I know you're too intelligent a man to pander to myth. But consider the black man who would come forward and admit to, say, having a small penis? That man doesn't exist; the reason he doesn't exist is because there is a point where that myth seems to serve us. For whites to believe black men their sexual superiors is to empower us in some subversive way. The thought of their resentment or fears of inadequacy is a source of power for us—one that can never really be acknowledged, except in a joke. But this joke permeates the culture and no one laughs as hard as we do. We really do pander to the myth, don't we? We might disown it publicly, but privately we accept it as a quiet truth. Ultimately it's depreciatory. It reduces us all to the Bestial Man. That's the trap of such delusion. At some point you have to wake up from the high-wire act of your cognitive dissonance to the fact that the net beneath you is made of smoke.

I think that could explain why it took me so long to acknowledge my problem. Even Paula bought it. Whenever my erections were slow to develop or semitumid, she would attribute it to stress or fatigue. Once, around the Christmas holidays, she even ascribed it half-jokingly to too much excitement. And because these lapses were only temporary we remained true to our fiction. But by the spring of last year I had begun to notice an increase in the frequency of problems. I'm sure Paula noticed it too.

One night we found we could no longer pretend. It was August by then; I remember the evening vividly. I was sitting downstairs in the TV room, dividing my attention between a rebroadcast of *Spartacus* and a fuzzy photocopied flier that had inexplicably appeared on my desk earlier that day. It read only CPT SEE QUARTER TILL, hand-scrawled in runny unsymmetrical letters. I remember thinking, Umph, there's something familiar here. But something at the sides of my neck distracted me—Paula's fingers, moving around to my chest in a cursive fluidness. Familiar, sublime in their confidence. A manner I've seen the blind use when glossing long pleasant sentences of Braille. She came around to face me, wearing only a lavender teddy, which she snapped open at the crotch with an effortless touch of her nail.

When I made it up to the bedroom, though, I couldn't get hard, not even partially. I hadn't expected it; everything seemed fine downstairs. The suddenness and severity of this episode unnerved me. It was different from the others. My fear came crushing down upon me. Was this the final stage in what had been a gradual decline? Paula kissed me and told me not to worry. "You put yourself under too much pressure," she said. "You just need to relax a little."

But I didn't really believe her. I suddenly wanted nothing more than to sleep, to fold myself into the darkness. She stroked my forehead and I dozed and dreamt a short fitful dream about the day we bought the Benz and went riding around the neighborhood. Only in the dream when I tried to enter the car the doors were all locked. Paula kept reminding me that the car was hers, as if I had been contesting that fact.

Later that night she tried to arouse me again—not against my will. But again no show, just limp dangling meat. And so there I was, right at the kernel of every male fear.

Paula was undaunted; she was lovingly determined to prove to me that my affliction was temporary. Perhaps she was answering some call to arms of feminine pride. (Perhaps it was more self-serving than any of that?) Over the next few weeks she began to experiment, first with her attire. Silk, satin, lace, leather—she even bought a pair of edible panties. Then the emphasis turned to technique. Exotic hand jobs, wildly theatrical blow jobs—which had never been a favorite activity of hers—done now with a particular...embouchure? There was also a bunch of devices—things you might find at the back of a dirty magazine—that all guaranteed results of some kind. You know, cock rings, pull-over vibrating rings, and a host of placebos with names like Pile Driver, Stay Hard, Rod Riser. After a while, when she saw that things weren't going to change, her attitude of gentle but dogged determination slowly faded. We moved into a new phase. At night she would climb in bed silently, finding me already under the covers. Sometimes we would go through the pretense of snuggling, only I would soon drift away in turns and starts until finally we would both be alone, staring into the darkness.

It was clear now that there would be no miracle cure, and my disposition changed radically. I won't try to explain it. What I could tell you would probably fall short of actuality. I will say that at times I would walk around the house too petulant and wired to ignore. In these instances Paula could only watch me with the supplicating glances women use as a vernacular. At other times the whole situation would seem to take on this crazy air of dreary solemnity. As if we were in mourning. A wake for a dead pecker. We would talk then, sometimes into morning. But no matter how much better I would feel, I'd soon slip back into petulance.

Then after a few weeks I wasn't even petulant anymore. I wasn't anything—just overcome, it seemed, by a warm somnolence. I can compare it now to taking Demerol in trace amounts. A perpetual state of consciousness somewhere between sleep and a sense of slow dissipation into elemental proportions. For the second time in our marriage Paula and I began to go to bed without speaking to each other. We ate together, slept together, went to work every day, but my senses seemed to operate from a new configuration, blunted and obtuse. Food had no smell; sleep brought little satisfaction. My Jag was just a red car, my best blazer a blue field of fabric that clung to my shoulders like swaddling. Only bourbon had a sensual presence. It burned my throat on the way down; it let me know it was there.

Eventually, though, I would find that there were some things that led to fresh perspectives, vistas of a beguilingly paranoiac and rancid vividness that once seen, once experienced, could never be forgotten. It began one evening in, of all places, our bed of pensive silence. Paula had her back to me and as I stared up into the ceiling, I heard her say quietly, "Billy, maybe you should see a doctor." For a second, just a second, I wasn't sure what she meant. I heard her clearly, but she almost seemed to be saying something else, something sarcastic about me. But as I said, it only lasted a second.

five

Do you recall meeting a relative of mine from Annapolis, my cousin Arleigh? I've been trying to remember this morning exactly when you would have met him. Do you remember Arleigh at all? He's a cousin on my mother's side, a Williams. His visits to Roberts were fairly infrequent since his parents, my Aunt Otelia and Uncle Rudy, weren't bound to my grandmother by blood but rather by an obedience to the soundness and necessity of tradition and etiquette. That a modicum of respect and fellowship for all relations was expected, no matter how slack the blood tie, and we could generally count on Arleigh's family to visit once or twice a year. I think you first met Arleigh the year his brother Delroy went into the army. In fact I'm certain of it because Arleigh would not let us forget about his brother in the army that day. It was in the spring; Arleigh would have been about eight or nine and you and I fifteen or sixteen. I wanted to throw the football around, but you and Arleigh discovered a mutual interest in science and bookish things. We went to your house so Arleigh could see the scrapbook you'd put together on the Mercury launches and your book about Jacques Cousteau. That's when I saw the body-builder magazine you had stuffed between your bed and the wall. You didn't know I'd seen it, much less picked it up and leafed through it, since you and Arleigh were so engrossed in the scrapbook that you'd forgotten all about me. I think you'd forgotten that the magazine had been left there because later when I asked you about it (just as a joke really, I didn't think anything of it then) your face twisted into a nervous little smile and your eyebrows arched up. I had seen every expression your face could form, and to see embarrassment, so unexpectedly, left me feeling deceived somehow. I couldn't entirely account for it. I guess it was because I'd never before felt that you had held anything back from me. It was the first time I'd ever considered that there were things about you I wasn't allowed to know. It put me on my guard. I didn't openly acknowledge it, but I didn't quite believe you when you told me you were planning to lift weights next year in preparation for senior football, and that the magazine was kind of a study aid. I didn't bother to point out what you already knew yourself, that you had never before so much as mentioned football in all the time I'd known you. Why I never pursued the matter further is still something of a mystery to me.

But what's the point of all of this now? I'd begun to tell you about Arleigh only because he was the physician I called at Paula's suggestion. I thought I could talk to him discreetly to collect a little information, as preface to whatever my next course of action would be. You wouldn't believe the part of fortune my little cousin has acquired as Dr. Arleigh Williams. He's a big-time specialist in internal medicine with a thriving practice in downtown Annapolis. But I guess success has its price. He's no longer on the best of terms with his parents because he chose to marry a white woman—the rebellious daughter of some uppity cracker family from South Carolina.

Arleigh ended up at Duke on a basketball scholarship. You don't follow sports so you probably wouldn't have heard of him. He was known as the R Man, with the double entendre for his incredible rebounding skills. Actually, he wasn't that good. He was never approached by anyone from the NBA. He stuck with his original intention to become a physician and, I suppose, to marry Iris, the girl he had met down there. He finished medical school at the University of Maryland and did his internship at Hopkins. Afterward he opened the Annapolis practice. His timing was impeccable, since Annapolis was just beginning to sell off its grubby tidewater rusticity for a more brass-plated, tourist-souled quaintness. It's evolved into a fashionable diversion from the marble and monuments of Washington, just an hour down Route 50. I don't think Arleigh's quick success has startled anyone more than himself. He and Iris have a big house, and I'm told marginal acceptance, in their Sherwood Forest community. Then there's his forty-two-foot sloop in the downtown marina ("and," Paula would scoff, "a white wife"). Anyway, I phoned Arleigh.

His receptionist took my call. "Dr. Williams's office," she answered.

"Is he available?"

"He's with a patient now, sir. Do you want to make an appointment?"

"No, no thank you. This is his cousin; I just wanted to speak with him. Could you do me a favor and have him call Billy Covington when he gets a chance?"

"Okay, sir, that's Billy Cov-ing-ton. Is there a number?"

"He has it. Just tell him I'm at home."

I waited. More than anything impotence teaches the art of sublimation. On any normal Saturday morning, Paula and I would be upstairs making love, or shopping downtown at the harbor. But what do you do when you can't make love to your wife and buying has lost its appeal? I sat the phone beside my chair, closed the doors, poured myself a bourbon and water, and turned on the ball game. The Orioles and the Kansas City Royals. I came in on the bottom of the second inning, the O's at bat. It was near the last game of the season. When Arleigh returned my call it was the bottom of the sixth, the Birds were down by three, and I was on my fourth drink. Just drunk enough to know I had to act sober—something I've never had trouble pulling off.

"Hi, Billy. It's Arleigh." We exchanged the usual polite salutations. I asked about Iris; he asked about Paula. I may have attempted some ribald little irony about women in general, and I'm sure I asked about Uncle Rudy and Aunt Otelia. He brushed over that one and began to tell me about how busy he'd been and how sorry he was that he hadn't gotten back to me sooner.

"I think everyone in Annapolis had an ailment today," he said.

"And they all turned up in your office. What tough luck," I told him.

"Now listen to that. You're the one hobnobbing with the capitalists—with your big house in Roland Park no less."

"I just work for Varitech, I don't own it."

"Yeah, not yet anyway. So tell me, what can I do for you?"

"This is a little awkward," I began. "I need some information for a friend at work. He knew I had a rich doctor cousin and he wanted to be discreet. I thought you might be able to recommend a specialist for him. He's having trouble getting his pecker in gear."

"Stuck in neutral, huh? A friend you say? Hummm, I think I'm going to have a talk with Paula," he joked.

"I know how that must sound, but it's the truth. Besides who ever heard of an impotent black man? We're the studs of all studs, right?"

He laughed. "Well, statistically speaking, race doesn't seem to be much of a denominator. Male sexual equipment in general seems to be pretty tricky. Your friend could have any number of problems. I wouldn't even want to guess without knowing anything about him. I'd suggest he start with a urologist anyway. The guy I'll recommend is a personal friend. His name is Tyrone Chang—the only non-black person I've ever met named Tyrone. Besides that, he's good; we did med school together. He has an office right in downtown Baltimore, on Charles Street."

"An Asian, huh? Is it my imagination or are there fewer American doctors these days?"

"Relax, Billy, you're beginning to worry me! Ty's an American all right; born and bred in Boston. A card-carrying Republican. So tell your friend not to let those epicanthic folds worry him. He'll be in safe hands."

He laughed hard at that. (I wasn't sure what an epicanthic fold was.) My cousin enjoys no humor more than his own. The stuff about the Republicans was a special barb for me. I switched parties a few years back and Arleigh has never let me forget it. Although in truth he'd make a better Republican than I ever would. He gave me Dr. Chang's phone number and address and we chatted a little more about family and finally fishing. A conversation with Arleigh always closed on fishing. Neither of us had found the time to get down to Point Lookout that fall. The sea trout were said to be plentiful as far in as Cornfield Harbor. We decided to set up a trip soon, before the remainder of the season slipped past. We left it at that, like we'd done every fall. I don't think I've been fishing with Arleigh in four years.

Now I know what you're thinking: did he really buy that stuff about my friend with a problem? It was a lame opening line, I know. A drunken reflex, let's say. The often-seen scenario of an endless list of B-movies, no doubt. Clichés and contrivances come to us in forms unbeknownst even to ourselves. We use them as a shorthand to skirt around responsibility. They save us the trouble of thinking deeply. Donna says it's one thing that's brought us to our present state of "whoredom" (her term for the lack of commitment and self-definition in our modern world). I couldn't tell you for certain if Arleigh believed any of it or not. He never mentioned it again. You know, I'd ask him about it now, but he hasn't come to see me since I've been here.

I just noticed the clock. It's noon already. I had planned to start writing early this morning, just to pick up where I left off yesterday without missing a beat. But I woke up late. Can you believe it? I haven't been to work in almost seven months and I still wake up later on Saturdays than any other day of the week. Donna will be in with my lunch anytime now and then there's my therapy afterward. I'm being taught to walk again. If I have more time this evening, I'll write a little more.

six

One of the starlings stopped by to say hello this morning. I saw him perch on my windowsill and glare in at me with his mocking inky eyes, bobbing convulsively as he cackled. They're strangely handsome birds, really. Sometimes the morning sun will pool just beneath the camber of their wings in this dazzling panchromatic slick. Imagine those black wings having all that possibility. I don't know what keeps them here. This is their second try at building that nest. Donna and I watched the first one slide along the rainspout during a thunderstorm and drop three stories. But Mom and Pop Starling are back at it again. I called them Heckle and Jeckle at first, not realizing they were building a home and a family together. I think Heckle and Jeckle were magpies anyway. I haven't made up any new names, just Mom and Pop Starling.

I'm sorry I didn't have more time to write yesterday. Paula came by in the evening with another letter from her parents, actually her father. He sent a card this time. I don't think it was a Hallmark; I don't know for sure. I threw it away. Donna wanted me to keep it because she'd never seen black models on a greeting card, and because she thought that what Dr. Bond had written inside was "wise beyond the conventional wisdom." But I threw it out anyway. It would have only been another reminder of the disarray I had plunged everyone into. Both of the letters that have come to me here from Dr. Bond seem to follow a single theme. Dignity. He seems to think I should be like Dr. King and exploit my circumstances to bring forth something inspirational and trenchant, something like my version of "Letter from Birmingham Jail." What he actually said was that I "must find and use that little bit of strength we all keep hidden away for times like these." I'm sure he doesn't fully understand what happened. He thinks I should show more dignity. Not that he would come out and say that, but I know him well enough to read his words for what they mean to him. I wish it were as easy as he thinks, but dignity isn't a decision you make, it's something you take along with you, and it can manifest itself so differently in a given situation that you can become confused by its appearance.

I don't believe I could ever make Dr. Bond appreciate how difficult it is to sustain a sense of dignity in the corporate world—and stay employed. Men and women of Dr. Bond's generation see the doors open they fought to have opened and then look upon the likes of me with embarrassment. They have little understanding for what lies beyond that ivory threshold. Dr. Bond works for himself, a black man serving a grateful black community. They allow him a brevet standing and then look in awe upon the fruits of what they've tithed: the house, the German cars, the position as racial spokesman. His dignity is packaged in the communal strength of belonging to a culture that recognizes him as a native son. (For the culture that wouldn't recognize him, he has his library.)

I'm trying to think of an example, something that would make clear to you what I'm trying to say. Let's see, an example. Ah, yes. At a marketing Christmas party several years ago John Haviland asked me a question about Paula's parentage. He was evidently baffled over her toast complexion and recessive green eyes.

"She's a gorgeous woman. Arc both her parents black?" Haviland asked, with absolute innocent curiosity. John, Lloyd Harrow, and I were standing by the punch bowl watching Paula lead a growing group of slightly drunken executives and their wives through an a cappella rendition of "The Christmas Song." I could see Lloyd tensing up. He took a quick sip of his punch and looked away. He knew as well as I the risk Haviland had taken in asking his question. It was a broad opening to a deep well of unresolved emotion.

This would have all taken place right around the time I'd made my big splash with the corporate slogan. Haviland hadn't yet offered me a position in his organization, but he was making overtures. In fact it was he who had invited Paula and me to the party; I wasn't even part of marketing at the time. How would you have answered the question? I had the choice of simply answering yes, her parents were indeed black, or I could have added a little discourse on the all-too-widespread concubine status that many black slave women had held, that Thomas Jefferson himself was guilty of this, and that this practice accounts for the various skin and eye shadings of modern black Americans. I could have also pointed out that his apparent ignorance of this fact was evidence of the short shrift the black experience is given in the education and minds of Americans. I could have asked him why her parentage mattered at all. Any of these responses, delivered with or without a measure of tact, might have been given. But what, in your opinion, was the dignified answer? Should I have taken the question to task, or should I have looked at dignity as the more long-term benefit of guarding my tongue?

Well, what I did was answer the question. (Was there ever any doubt?) I had been coached on the answer my entire life.

"Oh yes, her parents are black. She's just very light complexioned. It's pretty common," was my reply. He almost seemed grateful for my answer and for my eagerness to answer. Haviland would never have asked another black that question. It was a measure of how comfortable he was becoming with me. And in the politics of large corporations careers are built on that kind of comfort. You see, it wasn't just a question. It had another importance. It was a way of confirming things—for him at least. For me, lying here today, it seems like the first step in a duel wherein I would eventually have to turn and stare myself in the face.

But I didn't understand any of that then. I went about building my career in Haviland's organization, cultivating my reputation as a team player. I became the one black man every white executive made sure they knew. Because you see, my name could be dropped. Knowing me was in a way a measure of one's fairness and open mind. A black employee who might have expressed concern about the lack of blacks in management would be told, "Well, Bill Covington seems to be doing okay. I see him pulling up here in a Jaguar every morning." I was like the black model who turns up in advertisements among a smiling group of whites, usually near the back in print ads, usually without a speaking part in television ads, but functioning in both as a symbol of some elusive mythical state of grace.

With my impotence came a slow fermenting paranoia that would gradually permeate every impulse my senses fed back to me. But I'm anticipating again. Yesterday I had started to tell you about Dr. Chang. I did eventually see him. I made the arrangements from my office early the following Monday. In fact, I was able to get an appointment that same day for one in the afternoon.

What I also found that day was another crude photocopied flier lying in the center of my desk. Same scrawl, same cloudy message: CPT SEE QUARTER TILL. I scanned the desktop for anything else that might have accompanied it, but there was nothing. I put it in the center drawer of my desk, where I promptly forgot about it. I had other less cryptic problems to address.

My secretary, Nancy Maruski, came in with some phone messages from late Friday.

"Good morning, Nancy," I said, glancing at the slips of paper as they were leaving her hand for mine. There were three messages: the top one from Carl Rice in graphic arts, then Stan Walsh from our ad agency, and finally Len Townes, the company's operations manager. "So," I said, looking up at her, "how was your weekend?"

"Oh, nothing special," she answered. "I went down to the harbor for breakfast after church on Sunday. I ate too much."

She was not so much looking at me as inspecting me, the way one might weigh the sturdiness of a chair before sitting.

"Oh," she said suddenly, as if the brief silence between us had become too loaded with innuendo. "You also had a call from Lloyd. I don't think I wrote that one down. He said it wasn't important."

"Why does he always call me here when he's only three steps down the hall?"

"He's a hard one to figure." She smiled. Lloyd had been flirting with Nancy since he arrived here. She seemed more surprised by his attention than anything else, as if she weren't sure he was actually addressing her. What made that odd was the fact that she was not an unattractive woman. She was a kind of graduated version of the type once seen all over at Point Lookout during the summer. We'd see them at gas stations or in the parking lots of liquor stores, always wearing tight Capri pants, always leaning across the hood of a red car of some kind, always with blond hair and dark roots, near-experimental eye makeup, a Winston in the corner of the mouth, perhaps a bottle of Coke in one hand. They'd laugh when their boyfriends yelled, "Hey, niggers!" as they passed us in a cloud of thundering dust and bitter smoking wheels. Yet as much as we despised them, there was something alluring about those women, a quality that was at once whorish and innocent. It's a niggerish thing to admit, I know, but I could have almost forgiven them for their choice of company, perhaps realizing in the vague inarticulate way of adolescent minds that they too may have been the descendant chattel of some other doomed race. (And on this subject Paula would say, "And that's exactly why black men like your cousin Arleigh marry white trash like Iris.")

She turned to leave my office and was halfway through the door when I called her back. "Oh, before I forget. I have an appointment downtown today. I should be back around three."

"I'll put it down," she said and she was gone.

My first call of the morning was to Carl Rice. (I'll have to tell you more about Carl soon.) He was putting together a flier for me on the Varitech national sales meeting. An event our marketing department sponsored every year for no other pressing reason than to make and renew acquaint-ances between the Varitech sales and marketing reps scattered around the country like dandelion seeds. Carl had bluelines of the fliers and wanted me to make one last approval before they went into print. I would have normally delegated a project this minimal to one of the two professionals who reported to me. But this job had come to me in the form of a memo from John Haviland himself. It was nothing more than a note attached to a copy of last year's flier. It read: "Bill, what can we do to spice up this year's program? Can you help?"

I told Carl I would be by at four o'clock. Nancy came in again with the morning mail. Dierdre Rosen was standing in the doorway behind her. She asked tentatively if she could speak to me. I asked her to have a seat. She was one of my two professionals, officially my executive assistant, which in the argot of Varitech meant that her position was a newly created one. As a service (and in the interest of political well-being), it was a tradition to further embellish the children of our executives by hiring them. In my office, only Nancy and I could claim no blood relatives in the company. Dierdre, however, could and did claim her father, Neil Rosen, our chief research scientist—a powerful man who made recommendations on funding for all the new product and marketing programs. ("The man who sitteth on the right hand of Haviland," Lloyd liked to remark.)

Dierdre called me in the spring last year, two weeks out of college. She identified herself ("You might know my father, Neil Rosen?"). She claimed she was only interested in seeing me for an informational interview, not as a preface to an actual job, but just as a "chance to see what the real job market is like." That's what she said. I saw her the next day; we talked for two hours. I took her to lunch. She left me a copy of her résumé. Standard stuff: school activities, aspirations, the full name in bold type, DIERDRE RUTH ROSEN.

But it had been the very last line that bolted my attention—a fully capitalized topic sentence that began VARITECH FAMILY and went on to list the names and office extensions of her father and a brother, Seth, who worked in engineering. I had never seen it so boldly put. With Gordy Gavin, my other professional, there had at least been a more progressive disclosure. Nothing in bold type. He had obviously received more instruction in just what corporate culture dictated in such situations (something more akin to a stray line injected into the conversation with a certain idle irony).

The day after my meeting with Dierdre, Neil called. I told him I was impressed with his daughter (which was true) but that my budget could not absorb a new employee. I mentioned that I was planning to request an increase in my department's funding. I hired Dierdre two months later. She's been an exceptional worker.

Looking at her that morning as she followed Nancy into my office, I could see she hadn't come in to chat—which she occasionally did. She still hadn't taken a seat. She just stood at the front of my desk—dead center. I guess it was some form of courtesy because when Nancy left the room she finally sat down.

"I'm having some real problems with Len Townes," she began abruptly, as if she were breaking into a conversation already in progress. "I don't think I can work with him."

"What kind of problems are we talking about?"

"Well, for one thing he's rude. A flaming rude ass . . . just phony."

"What else? That isn't much to go on."

"He won't let me do my job. I spent four weeks working on that wave-solder video—researching stock footage, having new footage taken. And the script; I must have done twenty drafts of that script just getting everybody happy with it. So what does he do? He calls a review meeting and shoots everything down. He told me I have no understanding of the business of this company—in front of everybody!"

"When was all this?"

"The review? End of the day Friday. I just sat there. It was so rude. He just tore the whole thing apart. I couldn't say a word."

"I wonder if that's what this is about?" I held up the phone message from Len. It startled her; she had been about to say something more. The phrase was being restructured now, decelerated.

"I'm sure it is," she said. There was a caustic edge to her voice now, no longer just tumbling indignation.

"I'll talk to Len. He's a very particular guy and there are a lot of them around here."

"It was just so unprofessional." She was caving in to diffidence. "He could have pulled me aside, or talked to me before the meeting."

"I'll find out what his problem is and we'll talk again. In the meantime just do what you were doing."

When she left, I phoned Len. He was between meetings but promised a return call later in the day. What I hadn't let Dierdre know was that my own opinion of Len wasn't very high. It's my belief that he wasn't too fond of me either, or Carl Rice, or Curt Reed, or Selma King, or any of *us* in management for that matter. I have no proof I could take to a court; it was more an attitude. It left no physical evidence and generally went undetected by the nonblack witnesses we most wanted to validate it (and of course without their validation nothing we saw existed).

There are some facts I could point to, but again any lawyer would tell you they don't prove anything in and of themselves. In his six years as operations manager, Len had never hired a black person to a supervisory level in his group. He'd never been able to find anyone with "the right background mix," he once told George Yardly, who was answering a grievance a machinist had filed against one of Len's shop managers. His answer had apparently satisfied everyone, including Haviland, since no further action was ever taken. Under his operations group Len had all the black machinists in the company. So officially the EEO office had no complaints with him.

Len knows no blacks personally ("But then," a lawyer might say, "neither do a lot of whites."). He has never known a black person socially ("Again, most whites don't. It's not a crime."). He lives in a neighborhood where no blacks live ("That's simple economics. And blacks segregate themselves."). He displays a disdain for most black politicians ("Party affiliation, so what?") and musicians like Stevie Wonder ("Really? Even 'Fingertips Part II'?"). He is still surprised that Reagan signed the King holiday into law ("What did he really do for America? There are blacks who don't think he deserves a holiday."). The only positive remarks I've ever heard Len make about anyone black concern either basketball or football ("What's there left to say about Jim Brown or Dr. J?"). Judging from the way Len expresses himself, he's just a regular guy, no different from most of the executives at Varitech.

But in his unreconstructed days, during which time I came to work for Varitech, Len was a very vocal opponent of the new affirmative-action program. Not that this stance, in and of itself, made him unique; it was his in-your-face style of expressing his beliefs that conveyed hostility. Once, while eating in the cafeteria, I heard him telling a colleague about the then-recent shooting of George Wallace out in

Laurel. The whole country was buzzing about it and Len had been right at the scene, close enough to hear the shots, to see Wallace fall and Bremer wrestled to the ground.

"I wish I could have gotten a hand on him," Len told his friend, knowing full well, I've always believed, that I was within earshot. "We thought for sure it was a nigger. I'm still not convinced it wasn't." This was Len Townes before his rebirth. The man whom I would be meeting later that day to discuss Dierdre's video project was a new person.

This was really a fairly typical morning for me. Most of my time was spent on the phone assuaging people. I don't know if you have anyone in the academic world analogous to the marketing professional. They are the people I deal with most commonly. The best of them will give the impression of knowing nothing other than the intimacies of their products. It makes for tedious conversation. They express their desires to me for new brochures or ads with a polite but almost spiritual passion, like a mantra that begins "Our customers." But then that is their job— identifying markets, creating markets. It was just that I was finding it increasingly hard to deal with them. I couldn't stay focused. My mind would wander, lingering on any insignificance, anything to avoid hearing another word about "our customers." I found myself delegating more and more work to Dierdre and Gordy. I would ask Nancy to hold all of my calls and close myself up in my office, where I would dawdle the day away.

It was like that on the day I've described. First, I began to go through my mail. My letter opener was a gift Lloyd had brought back from a trip to Riyadh. A pigmy scimitar with a handle of inlaid ivory and calamander. And I thought: This blade is an incongruity. I ran my fingers across the tang—textureless stainless steel. Too uniform and seamless

57

a forging to mate the other-worldliness of the handle. Its beauty was in its imperfection, its approximation of symmetry. I thought of Peter O'Toole in a blazing white haik in *Lawrence of Arabia*; an infinity of sand, a smoky brown–magenta expanse; turbaned millions kneeling toward the Kaaba, to the very black stone heart of the temple. I moved the blade to what I thought was east. And before I knew it, most of the morning was gone.

Then the phone rang: once, twice. I heard Nancy pick it up. She came through the doorway, hesitated before she spoke. In her eyes I must have seemed momentarily possessed, gazing across the arced blade into the static of the corner.

"Bill, it's your doctor's office reminding you about your appointment today," she said.

I spent a half hour or so writing memos to various people in marketing—a habit I had recently begun. I rarely made phone calls anymore. In the memos I would almost routinely urge that the respondent follow up with either Gordy or Dierdre.

Then I prepared to leave for Dr. Chang's office. I put my coat on and then cleared off my desk. I put papers in neat stacks, mail in the out box, wrote reminder messages to myself on a canary yellow notepad that had the words NOW REMEMBER printed across the top of each page.

When I went to put the letter opener in the drawer, I confronted the flier again. I picked it up. There was still something familiar about it, some remnant of a memory commandeered through the passage of time. I wanted to ask Nancy about it. Perhaps she had seen someone come into the office; perhaps she had overheard something. I looked out to her desk but she had already left for lunch. So I folded the flier and slipped it into my breast pocket. Then I wrote a message on my notepad reminding me to ask her about the flier when I returned.

There was only light traffic until I got to Russell Street. Even after I had turned onto Pratt, I still hadn't noticed the tightening concourse until everything came to a stop just below Charles Street, my exit.

The traffic was coming from the convention center on the opposite corner. There was all kinds of activity branching out from the shadows of that glass and concrete facade. Charter buses, taxis, stretch limos, great masses of people with tiny plastic cards pinned to their lapels, scattered speckles of navy blue, the reluctant sheen of double-knit attire. It was obviously a trade show or convention, but which? The American Boat Show, The National Cat Owners Show, or was it a "Star Trek" convention? I got my answer when the light changed and the traffic lurched forward. I could now see the marquee above the entrance to the hall. It read: WELCOME AMERICAN VACUUM SOCIETY. I wasn't sure if it was a joke, a misprint, or a scientific group. But it seemed almost written for me, another sarcastic riddle like Paula's comment a few nights before about my seeing a doctor. But as I had done with her comment, I dismissed my wild musings about the sign and scolded myself for thinking crazy thoughts.

seven

For some reason Donna asked me a lot of questions about you this morning. I suppose it was because she saw me writing yesterday. I've told her about this journal, but until today she'd never made mention of it. This morning, though, she sat with me as I ate breakfast, looking out the window at the starlings working on their nest. Your name came out of nowhere.

"This Paul Walker," she said, still looking through the window. "Why have you changed your mind about contacting him after so many years? You send him the card and now you do this journal for him, why? Have you given any thought to why?"

It seemed a simple question at first, but I found I had no answer. Everything I thought to say was rendered inadequate by these enormous complexities I'd never before considered. I thought I'd begun this journal to answer your letters, but I guess I'm not as sure of that now. It isn't even that I wanted you to know what happened to me—I haven't talked to anyone about that, not even Dr. Theodore. But I couldn't answer her question. My only response was a reluctant shrug. She picked up my tray and would have left the room without another word had I not asked her to explain herself.

"I wanted to see if you knew why," she said simply. See what I mean? She's spooky; just like I told you. She's a real spooky sister.

I think yesterday I'd left you on the way to Dr. Chang's. I'll never forget his office. The waiting area reminded me of an exhibit at an interior design exposition. It was all white, everything: the ceiling, the rough pargeted walls, the blond oak floors, the odd but distinctive overstuffed furnishings. (Could the impotence business have been this lucrative?) I hesitated at the door, preferring first to peer in through a low window. The only other person I saw was a slender redheaded woman—slightly discordant and yet provocative against all that white, like a Monk composition. She sat at the far end of the room, appearing all the more tiny and shrunken against the soft billowy massiveness of the couch. She was skimming through a magazine that had a picture of Yasir Arafat on the cover. I caught her glance as I came through the door. It was a quick, thorough assessment. Then she went back to the magazine, satisfied, it seemed to me. Could a glance have revealed so intimate and vital a thing? Or was my being here enough? What else could she have thought but that I was another impotent man? Even knowing that urologists do more than treat impotence didn't altogether ease the devouring paranoia I was beginning to feel.

A nurse emerged from a hallway to take a place behind the white semicircular counter that sat in the middle of the room. Her eyes were two solid black beads that seemed to rise from her dun skin like a liquid suspended in an emulsion. The name plaque pinned to her white smock, just above her right breast, read P. Chainsukh. She spoke with a thick indeterminable accent. It wasn't Indian or Arabic as I had expected. Several times during the discussion of the Blue Shield coverage, I had to ask her to repeat herself. When we were finished, she instructed me to have a seat.

"Doctier Chong will be wit you in a mooment," she said.

I took a seat opposite the redhead. She was reading a magazine called *Arab World*. I shot speculative glances in her direction, trying to solicit the look I thought I'd seen earlier. But she didn't (or wouldn't) look up at me. Not even when the nurse called my name and escorted me back to the examination area. I followed her down the short narrow hallway, stopping to squeeze past a man making his way out. (The redhead's husband?)

"I'll be wit you in a mooment, Mistier Donnell," she said to him. He nodded without a word. She pointed me to a door on the left and handed me a little plastic cup. "We need a ureen sampool. Try to feel de cop pleaze. Just seat it here when you are trugh"—she pointed to a tiny recessed set of shelves above the toilet—"and go to de room at de end ov de hol wheen you have done." Not quite an order, definitely not a request, but pleasant somehow in its economy. I filled the cup and went to the end of the hall.

When she returned she took my blood pressure and my temperature. She asked me some questions and jotted the answers down on a prepared form. One of the answers I gave was an outright lie. Before she left, she gave me a gown to put on. Soon afterward Dr. Chang entered, smiling, a clipboard under his arm. He was taller than I had expected, a good solid six feet. When he introduced himself and extended his hand I was almost too dumbfounded to respond. Arleigh hadn't told me about the accent. He had mentioned Boston, but I just hadn't made the association. It was uncanny, an accent that could have belonged to one of the Kennedys—but even his politics were wrong for that.

As we shook hands another more ominous thought gripped me. Could it be possible that Dr. Chang recognized my name from some past conversation with Arleigh? Arleigh might even have called to tell him that he had recommended a friend of his cousin Billy's. In either case my hopes for anonymity would have been futile. Dr. Chang did not act as if he was familiar with my name. I kept looking for some sign, but there were no answers in his eyes.

He pulled a stool up to the examination table. "I see here," he said, looking at the clipboard, "that you're having prostate trouble. Is this the diagnosis of another physician?"

He seemed truly puzzled. And he should have been. This was the lie I had given to P. Chainsukh. It was now time to fess up. "Well, no, I haven't seen another doctor. Your nurse asked me what I was here to see you about and, well, I guess I got a little embarrassed. I'd think it would be embarrassing for any man."

"What would?" he said.

"Impotence," I said with a false bravado. "I haven't been able to have an erection for more than a month now." I went on to give him a brief history of my problem.

"Do you ever have partial erections, in the morning maybe?" he asked, glancing down at the clipboard.

"Not anymore. For a while I did, but now nothing at all."

He scribbled something else down, then he asked me about my job and if I was under any unusual stress there.

"Nothing out of the ordinary," I said.

"You are married, Mr. Covington?"

"Yes."

"How long?"

"Fourteen years."

"Any unusual stress or problems there?"

"Just the impotence. I don't think a problem can be its own cause, can it?" He ignored the question.

"And you've never had any problem before now?"

I told him how the impotence seemed to have developed over the last six or seven months. Prior to that, I added, I had been like the proverbial sports car. "You know, you want more speed all you do is push the accelerator down farther." He smiled in a labored pleasant way this time. The way doctors smile when they want to instill comfort and keep the patient on task. What he really wanted me to do was answer his questions.

"How much alcohol do you consume on a daily basis?"

"Maybe two drinks before dinner. Maybe a beer at lunch. What does that have—"

"We'll go into that a little later. Do you ever engage in any sexual practices that might leave your penis sore for any length of time?"

"The kinkiest thing I've ever done was leave my sunglasses on once."

He didn't even smile this time. "Any history of kidney or heart problems?"

"No," I said flatly. I resigned myself to follow his style from here on.

"How about your parents, any heart or kidney troubles?"

"I really don't know. They were both killed when I was six. I don't know anything about their medical histories."

"How about your brothers or sisters?"

"There's just me."

He changed his format for the last few questions. I would say he almost seemed uncomfortable. He had barely lifted his eyes from the clipboard the entire time we'd been speaking. But now he put the clipboard aside and looked at me directly.

"You know, Mr. Covington, sometimes a man can have problems of this nature with a wife but be fine with someone else."

It was my turn to be direct. "Is that a question?"

"Sometimes impotence can be brought on by, well, boredom."

"You're asking me two questions, right? Do I have a mistress and am I impotent with her?"

He sighed and attempted a quick smile. "This is always a difficult thing for me to ask. Most of my patients aren't as direct as you seem to be. I sometimes have to finesse my answers out of them."

The idea of this man showing finesse of any kind was truly funny. "Well," I said, "I don't have a mistress. I don't fool around on my wife. My problem has nothing to do with desire. I just can't get it up."

He nodded, picked up the clipboard, and turned it over in his lap. "Are there any questions you would like to ask me? I'm sure you must have some." His tone was almost conciliatory.

"What are my chances of getting this thing straightened out?"

"Well," he said, eyebrow raised, quizzical shrug, "it's difficult to say. You're in good health. There are things in your favor."

"Statistically speaking then, how many men with impotence are cured?"

"Any number I could give you would be misleading."

"You're confusing me. You ask me if I have questions and then you evade them."

He smiled again, a quick bleached-bone flash. "Please

understand," he said. "I'm not trying to be evasive. It's just your questions don't have cut and dried answers. A cure, for instance, can mean different things to different people. One man might consider a semirigid prosthesis a cure; another might consider it unacceptable. As for statistics the only thing that I've seen that's been reliably quantified has to do with diabetics. We know that there are roughly ten million nationwide and that about half of them are impotent."

"All right, all right. So what happens now; what's next for me?"

"Tests. We do tests. It's the only way to isolate the problem. We must investigate everything. Your problem might be some part of a larger disorder."

"Larger disorder?"

"Your problem could be purely psychological or it could be part of a larger physiological disorder."

"Like what?"

"That's what the tests will tell us."

We both smiled that time. "Well, what will we be looking for?"

"For starters any constrictions in your vascular system. On one level an erection is a matter of blood flow and blood pressure. The IVP studies will tell us how efficiently your blood is moving through your kidneys and testicles. We'll do a testosterone study, a CBC, a penile nerve conduction study, an NPT. There are a few more. Most we can do right here. The NPT will have to be done in the sleep lab down at University Hospital."

"NPT?"

"Nocturnal penile tumescence. It's to see if you're having erections in your sleep."

"What would it mean if I were?"

"It might suggest some psychological or emotional cause

for your impotence. If you're not having them the problem is probably organic."

"What will we do if the problem is psychological?"

"There are avenues to take—some new developments. But we're getting ahead of ourselves. First we do tests. The entire workup will take about three months. I'll have Pregna schedule your next appointment and we can begin then."

"Well, I'd like to get going as soon as possible."

"Good. Today you just get a physical. Very routine. I'll need a blood sample."

Every profession has its own jargon—an easy presumptive way of expressing things. Mastering it is itself an indication of a certain prowess, however real or contrived. I had been impressed with Dr. Chang, not for his bedside manner (which was close to nonexistent) but for his dexterity at bouncing acronyms.

After I was dressed and prepared to leave, he reminded me to schedule my next appointment with "Pregna." P. Chainsukh had a name now. Still nothing I could put on a map. Her accent was like a conglomeration of several tongues. With her help, I scheduled my next appointment.

"So lon," she said as I walked out.

The phrase hadn't made immediate sense so I only smiled and nodded.

Outside the wind had picked up, a little cooler than the air that had come through a week earlier. It signaled the end of Indian summer, which meant we would soon be visited by the cold late-fall rains that habitually besiege Maryland. It's always seemed a melancholy time of year, and so it was particularly appropriate that I should associate it with my own sense of falling away—autumn as the theme of my mental egression. I think this was the first time I acknowledged my uncertainty. Dr. Chang had prescribed a course of action that at least promised answers, and that was exactly what I was beginning to fear.

Before my visit to Dr. Chang the weight of my impotence was in some way buffered by possibility, by hope—no matter how fanciful. Every answer, every discovery he now made would delimit that possibility, reducing it eventually to stark-naked absolute fact. I wanted to run to his office and tell him to forget the tests, to forget the whole thing. My tie streamed over my shoulder, beckoning me back it seemed. But I began to walk, south along Charles—against the flow of traffic—past the bars, the professional offices, the eclectic collection of small businesses and ethnic restaurants, then across Madison Street to Mount Vernon Place, where Charles divides itself.

At one time, this area was the home of Baltimore's aristocracy. Railroad magnates, land barons, importers of silk and spice—old money by the turn of the century. What remains here now is like a tribute to nineteenth-century sensibility and virtue. A confluence of French, Italian, and romantic Greek architectural styles—cobbled streets, regal green-rusting statues of local heroes long forgotten, a pocked multispired church, and the nation's first monument to George Washington. A 250-foot marble specter, rising in a smothered renown against the backdrop of the modern city like a lighthouse in the desert. It gives the place a doleful gravity, as if the whole area had been built to ward off some evil leaching from the underbelly of the culture. I felt like a trespasser, traveling through in disguise.

The sidewalks were crowded with businesspeople returning from lunch. I carefully took my place among them, wisking past fey, lead-skinned bag ladies and vacant teenaged kids with Goodwill clothing and sixty-dollar haircuts—like some comic machinations of the welfare state. I continued my play of indifference until a black woman with two small children approached me on the sloping sidewalk along the Walters Art Gallery. Both boys were preschool age; the woman didn't look more than twenty. She moved at an impatient pace, hurried and deliberate, like a tourist looking for the right street. The boys were presenting a problem. She had to stop every few feet to wait for them to catch up. They were playing a game that involved touching everything they passed. It kept them lagging behind the woman, tripping, stumbling, and laughing as they went. This time when they caught up with her she leaned toward the largest boy and swung—a quick openhanded jab that caught him square in the back of the head.

"I'mah slap the shit outta y'all if y'all don't come on!" she screamed. She raised her hand to the youngest boy, who tried to scramble away, but she grabbed his arm and pulled him to her. "You want some too?" she said. He shook his head; he was trying not to cry. "Well come on den."

I watched the three of them, the boys quiet and sullen now, disappear into an alley farther down Charles.

■   ■   ■

Lloyd Harrow was standing in the doorway of my outer office when I returned. He was speaking to Nancy in French.

"*Tu es le phénix de beauté,*" he said. I tapped him on the shoulder and he swung around.

"How long have you been standing there?" He smiled. Lloyd was always smiling.

"Don't worry, I don't know any French." Nancy got up from her desk, blushing just a bit. She began to read off my urgent phone messages, passing the slips to me as she did.

"Len Townes called for you," she said, handing the last slip to me. "It sounded important. And that call from Carl Rice, he wants to know if you can come by sometime around three-thirty today." She had another slip crumpled in her hand, which she gave to me. "And this one's from him," she said, pointing to Lloyd with a look of satiric impatience.

"Well, now I know how I'm thought of by marketing communications," he said. "What do you say about me when I'm not here?"

"*Mais tu es toujours ici!*" I replied.

"I thought you didn't know any French?"

"Was that French?" I said.

I really haven't told you much about Lloyd Harrow, have I? To this day I'm not sure what to make of him. He still seems to me like some random agent of fate—like the fool in *King Lear*. That sounds a bit inflated, I know, but Lloyd defies conventional explanation. I know now that during my association with him he was battling his own quiet demons. Did I mention that he was the son of a very wealthy stockholder—a scion of an old monied Philadelphia family—and that his position as John Haviland's executive assistant was a curious arrangement? Often the gofer of a powerful man has commensurate authority by virtue of that association. But he enjoyed no such stature. It was such a glaring anomaly. He was tall, blond, blue-eyed, and rich. Varitech should have been a virtual dukedom for him, yet he was generally not taken very seriously, and for good reason. He seemed to take little seriously himself. Of course, that only contributed to the aura of mystery that surrounded Lloyd. If he didn't crave power and didn't need money, why was he at Varitech? He had showed up two years and two months ago and had immediately assumed a position at Haviland's side. There was no formal announcement; he just appeared one day at a staff meeting. I later found out from a contact in personnel that he had been a sales manager in the Philly office. Descending from sales manager to executive assistant could only mean a disaster of some kind had taken place. But to my knowledge that was never discussed by anyone at Varitech.

Stranger still to me was Lloyd's seemingly self-imposed outsider status. He eschewed the avenues and comradeships easily accessible to most white executives. He associated with very few people, rarely talked about work when he did; he seemed to wander the plant dropping by various offices, mine most notably, usually delivering the most baffling and preposterous inanities. Usually, I said. Because Lloyd was also privy to information that I could have never otherwise obtained. Being close to Haviland, he knew things known by perhaps only three others in the plant. Sometimes he would come by and tell me all. I'm not entirely sure why. I'd like to think it was because he thought of me as a friend. But who's to say? I guess the problem is I didn't know Lloyd as well as I had once thought. That's something I've come to realize lying here. I knew things about him, but I don't know if that really goes toward explaining his behavior. He seemed to use obliqueness and flippancy as a way to keep people off balance. He never gave you the chance to ask him anything of importance. It was more than a fear of closeness. There was something he said once; I'm taking it out of context here, but he said, "I've already spent more time here than people who've retired and gone." Of course, another problem was that as my paranoia grew I was less sure of anything Lloyd, or anyone else, told me.

That afternoon we went into my office and Lloyd instantly lit a cigarette and began rummaging through a stack of trade magazines I had piled to the side of my desk. He got up and closed the door behind me.

"Did you hear about the black guy who found a bottle on a beach with a Jewish genie in it?" he said.

"I guess I will now."

"The genie said, 'I'll grant your any wish.' And the black guy says, 'Hum, you know what I'd really like? I'd like to be white and surrounded by pussy.' So the genie made him a tampon!" He paused for a roar of laughter. Like my cousin Arleigh, Lloyd was his own best audience. "Now you see," he said, "the moral of this story is, with a Jewish genie there's always a string attached!"

We both laughed. It was actually a little better than what usually came out of Lloyd's mouth. But I had to believe that he understood the joke had implications for me personally. Was he trying to tell me something? Nancy stuck her head in quickly to say that Len Townes was at a meeting but that he would call me as soon as he got back.

"You've got some secretary there," Lloyd said after she closed the door.

"Is that what you were telling her in French?" I hung my blazer up on the hook on the door and took a seat behind my desk.

"She didn't know what I was saying," he said, leaning back in the chair. "You know, Bill, I think something's bothering you."

"I think you should lighten up on the French lessons," I said.

"Such hostility," he came back, in his best Woody Allen voice. "What are you getting so upset about? This is chicken shit."

"How do you think it looks, you leering in my doorway speaking French to my secretary?"

"Not as bad as it would if you were doing it." He began chuckling.

"Come on, Lloyd; a couple of weeks ago I heard you out there telling her how ducks mate." He laughed harder at that than he had at his joke. "People are going to start wondering what's going on here."

"Honest to God, Bill, you worry like a goddamned old woman." He was still laughing but was making a weak effort to act serious. "No one's watching you, Bill; no one's assembling a file on you. I'd tell you if they were. You're paranoid, that's all." He shook his head trying to suppress a chuckle I knew was there. He took a last drag on the cigarette, pinched the end with two moistened fingers, and flicked the butt into the trash can like a spent cartridge. "You know, I came in here to tell you about my course. But I'm wondering if you want to be seen with me now, unsavory character that I am."

I sat staring back at him, anticipating something bizarre. "Well?"

"It was called managerial tactics. In my present high-pressure position as the manager of special projects, Haviland thought the course would be good for me."

"Is that what he said, really?"

"Not word for word, but you know, he went through the motions."

"All right, so far so good," I said. "Go on."

He began to laugh, anticipating himself this time. "Well you see, the whole thing was held outdoors, in the middle of the woods in this really remote part of Georgia—Bascove or Bascome, I think it was called. Of course you don't know any of this when you sign up."

"All right, all right, there you go! I knew this was coming sooner or later—the BS clause. There's always at least one in these stories of yours. You want me to believe that this course was held out in the woods? Come—"

"I'm telling you the truth, Bill! I always tell you the truth, you just don't see it," he said, laughing. "The flier only mentioned the Bascome Conference Center. It wasn't until you paid your seven-hundred-dollar registration fee and got off the plane in Atlanta that you realized you'd been slightly misled. There's this guy standing in the airport holding a sign that says BASCOME CONFERENCE CENTER. Now, I really didn't think anything strange about that; it says in the course description that you would be chauffeured to the conference center. But when everybody had to pile into this Chevy van outside the terminal, the light started to go on—you know what I mean? We drive for what seems like hours to what looks like a run-down fishing lodge. The driver gets out and introduces himself as Earl Pratt, 'your DI for managerial tactics.' "

The phone rang. I listened for Nancy to pick it up. She buzzed me on the intercom.

"It's Len Townes," she said. "He wants to know if you can come by in ten minutes."

I let her know that was fine, looking Lloyd in the face as I spoke into the speakerphone.

"Old Len," Lloyd said, almost to himself. "Old fat Leonard." He was grinning this nasty-little-boy grin, chuckling softly to himself.

"What?"

"I heard something funny about old Len today." He

was still chuckling. "You know Len's a Born-Again, don't you?"

"Yeah, but I've never seen him get carried away with it."

"Well, do you know his wife—ex-wife now, I guess?"

"I don't know her. I know who she is. She works in purchasing, right?"

"Yeah. Doris. Gorgeous woman. She could crush my skull with those long legs of hers any time. She's an aerobics fanatic." (I smiled. There were golden moments when it was possible to forget about my impotence.) "She's been dating George Yardly for the last six months and according to George, she has some tales to tell about our fat friend Len."

"I didn't know you socialized with George."

"Socialized? He *is* the HR manager so we do talk from time to time. He also has an XJ12 that he's rebuilding; immaculate body, but the engine's shot to shit. Anyway, he was telling me that Doris had a few stories to tell about Len."

"You said that already. Get on with it." I glanced down at my watch.

"Well, see, the first few months she and Len were separated they tried to get back together a few times and patch things up—which I still can't understand. What could she see in Len? Talk about bottom of the food chain. But whatever the reason, they get back together for a short time, right? So their first night back together Len wants flesh, and I don't mean no communion wafer either. I'm talkin' major pussy. So they go at it okay. Old Len gets his heart rate up—can you see it, can you imagine the sight? I mean it must've looked like a whale trying to hump a dolphin. But okay, Len's going for it, right? Well before long he starts whispering things to Doris in the heat of passion."

"Things? You mean religious things?"

"No, no, no. Len's a romantic—I mean things like 'fuck me baby.' Those kinds of things."

"I thought everyone did that." I smiled.

"No Bill; not white men," he responded, on the verge of laughter again. "Let me finish this before you have to leave! Okay, the next morning Doris wakes up—probably with a few fractured ribs—and what do you think she sees? There's old fat Leonard kneeling at the side of the bed, asking the Lord to forgive him for what he said!"

"Come on Lloyd, I—"

"And it's all true," he said. "It's bad enough Len's got chapped lips from kissing Haviland's ass up and down the halls. But this; that pitiful bastard. If I had a woman like Doris, I'd be on my knees thanking Jesus! Man those legs must go straight up to the loveliest—"

"All right, time to leave. I'll be late for 'old Leonard' if I don't get out of here. You'll have to finish telling me about your course, about Deliverance 101, some other time."

"Hey, I like that; Deliverance 101. You know, there's supposed to be another course along the same line in New Jersey somewhere, only there they give you these guns that fire paint pellets. It's like a corporate commando thing; you run around in the woods trying to hunt the other guys down. It's the latest thing in executive training."

I shook my head. Training for what? I wondered.

"You don't have to believe me," he said, still laughing. "I saw it on "Evening Magazine" last night. Oh yeah, before I forget: you do know that the British car show is this week-end, don't you?"

"No, I didn't. Has the year spun around that quickly? Damn, where does the time go?"

"It's here again all right, in Bowie, just like last time. But they're expecting two thousand people to turn out this year. Interested? Last year was pretty fun."

"Yeah, it was. I'll give you a call on Friday. I don't know what plans Paula has made already." We had moved out into the hall now. "I'll have to give you a call," I said.

"Sure, that's good," he said. He darted his head back around the doorjamb. "*Au revoir*," he whispered to Nancy. Then he looked back at me and smiled as he crossed the hall to his office.

I walked away from Lloyd like I usually did, wondering what had just occurred between us. It almost goes without saying, Paul, that everything I'm telling you here is recounted from memory. I don't think I've missed much; in fact, forgetting any detail of what happened is something I have been unable to do. But I'm no longer sure that I'm in a position to make interpretations. The point at which my perceptions began to deteriorate is not as clear as I had once thought. How can you really know when actuality has faded into paranoia or delusion when even the things that would have given you bearing are suspect?

Let me tell you about Len Townes. He was on the phone when I walked in past Charlotte, his secretary, who was also on the phone and so only gestured me along. Len stood as I entered, motioning me to take a seat. He was not a tall man. Not really much over five foot eight, but he was easily a 250-pounder. Most of it seemed to girdle his middle, an indeterminate gelatinous mass that rose from his shirt when he sat as if it were alive, feigning escape. His weedy red hair and smooth pink face made him look for all the world like a mutant cherub plucked from some forgotten sixteenth-century ribald painting.

At business meetings he was always careful to make what had become a trademark jocular self-deprecating comment, something like, "That sale is about as likely as me losing forty pounds by tomorrow." It was only one of the devices Len employed to maneuver around the brackets of that strange urbane prejudice we reserve for fat people. He must have known what people thought when they saw him—the polite repugnance, the quiet awe of his grotesqueness, an assumption of mental and physical indolence. Yet instead of attempting to divert attention from it, he eased the spectators into indulging their prejudice. He's gotten very good at it over the years. (But it wasn't always this way. I had once glimpsed at least a fragment of the true Len Townes, the one standing behind all the guile. That Len Townes was a man choking on his contempt for a great many things: on his rivalrousness, on his envy, on his longing to be in control.) Len's voice was another of his great deceits. It had this monotone avuncular sincerity. You half expected him to break into a discussion on fly-fishing, or the merits of home cooking, at any moment.

When he put down the receiver he thanked me for coming by. He wasted no time getting to the videotape, insisting that we view it first before discussing its problems. It was typical of the tapes we were regularly called on to produce, the usual overstated, single-minded excursion into the corporate ego. Dierdre had done a fine job considering the limitations of budget and subject.

All Len claimed he'd wanted was a little two-minute pitch that the sales guys could take around on calls.

"Something that shows the breadth of our manufacturing operation; you know. But I guess Ms. Rosen had other ideas." He handed me a copy of what he called a list of inaccuracies. In a surge, I remembered the flier tucked in the breast pocket of my coat. CPT SEE QUARTER TILL. I hadn't asked Nancy about it; I hadn't even remembered to look at the notepad I'd written the reminder message on.

Len sat in his seat looking over his list of Dierdre's infractions like a judge in traffic court. "How 'bout if I just let you handle these things here. It's really more your bailiwick than mine, anyway." He put the list aside. "I guess I see a larger problem here that I want to nip in the bud...I mean the way this whole project was run. It shouldn't have come down to me making a list and calling you in here." He paused, making sure I saw the smile, the benign chubby face, heard and believed the disarming voice. "Something's got to be done about that gal of yours, that Ms. Rosen. She's something else." Another pause and smile—almost a chuckle—as if he wanted me to believe that there was something subtly comic in what was being said.

"Anything I asked for in this tape was excluded," he continued. "Now, I've got to believe that some of that was done out of pure spite, plain and simple. I don't claim to be an expert in producing videos, but you'd think I'd have some say in a project that I'm funding. I don't think your gal has an appreciation for that." The entire time he talked, his voice never betrayed him. There was no elevation in his tone, no heat, just the same genial flatness. "I don't know what she had in mind," he added. "But just because her daddy can run roughshod over my department's budget...I still have a say in how I spend the money I do have. I'll tell you something, Bill, and you can say what you want, but I've never met a Jew that didn't think they were better than everyone else." There wasn't the slightest change of inflection in his voice; we could have been discussing the Orioles' latest home game. It was true—Len Townes could detach his voice from any context, his auto-ventriloquism keeping the audience fixed on the jolly fat mannequin and all but unaware of the man upon whose knee it sat. (But was I much better? He was speaking in a language that, as I told you, I also knew fluently. So how did I respond?)

I assured him that I would see that the things on his list were taken care of.

"And in the meantime," I added, "I'll have a little talk with Dierdre. We'll get things straightened out."

Len nodded. He wasn't working through any mental pother now. Why should he have been? He had exorcised his demon and it hadn't been Dierdre at all; it had been her father. I never got the specifics of it all.

Whatever it had been, it was over the moment I assured Len that Dierdre would be properly scolded. (I never said anything to her.) He took a stagey glance at his watch and announced in the same sustained and level voice he'd used our entire time together that he had a meeting to rush off to. He was already late, he declared. He thanked me again for coming by once we were out in the hallway and then he turned and left. I watched him bound down the corridor and I tried to picture him on his knees that morning, asking for the Lord's forgiveness. What would he have said—"Forgive me Lord for the fuck-me-baby stuff"? That might have been a topic of conversation to explore with Lloyd. But I had another appointment that afternoon, where I would find more corporeal things to discuss.

I must tell you now about Carl Rice. I had told him earlier that day to expect me at three-thirty. But it was past four when I finally arrived. The plant had so thinned out that I wasn't certain he would even be in his office. But there he was, at his desk reading—a half-eaten Hershey's bar in one hand, a steaming cup of black coffee in the other. There were several empty cans of Coke in the trash. I had something clever in mind to say, something about a caffeine IV being more immediate. But as I crossed the threshold into his tiny office, I stopped dead and then rushed over to his desk and snatched away the piece of paper he'd been reading. He flinched.

"Hey, what's with you?" he blurted out.

It was too late. I had the paper in my hand. It was also a photocopy, but I stood there reading it anyway—trying to make absolutely certain it was identical to mine. It was, of course; I'd seen the writing from the doorway. CPT SEE QUARTER TILL.

eight

It occurred to me today that you might not have heard about my grandmother. I've been thinking about her a lot lately. I know you had asked about her in one of your earlier letters. Well, she died near the end of my first semester of college.

I got the message from Uncle Rudy, who had been contacted by Dr. Richardson. She died in her sleep of a massive stroke. Quick and painless, Dr. Richardson later told me. She never regained consciousness.

Her body had gone undiscovered for almost two full days before Mr. Raymond Hines stopped by at his wife's urging. Mrs. Francine was sure something was wrong since she hadn't seen my grandmother since church on Sunday.

The day after he called, Uncle Rudy picked me up in front of Ritchie Coliseum in his new white Ford Fairlane. Aunt Otelia came along too. Her eyes were puffy and moist and I remember thinking that she had probably cried all the way from Annapolis to College Park. It had been a year especially littered with grief. Their oldest son, my cousin Delroy (the "big brother" in the army you had heard Arleigh speak of almost two years earlier), had been killed eight months before in a place called the Ia Drang Valley. So I pondered Aunt Otelia's tears, wondering which were for my grandmother and which were really Delroy's, and wondering too if there is ever a point at which anguish consolidates itself into one neat manageable emotional space. I rode in the backseat of the car with Arleigh, who must have been close to eleven by that time. He was still the bookish little boy you'd no doubt remember. On this day though he was a little timid. I think all the death had made him uncertain about what to say or do, or probably even how he should feel. He never said a word during the entire trip, but kept his face buried in successive issues of *National Geographic*. He read them all cover to cover.

I stayed in Roberts for three weeks. People sent flowers and letters of condolence. There was even a short painful note from your mother in Alabama. Uncle Rudy took care of the funeral arrangements but had to leave right after the burial. It was all the time away from work he could afford. He had arranged, before he left, to have Norris Gambrill (that old white lawyer you used to call "the Negroes' friend" because he had always taken black clients) stop by sometime soon. He also made me promise to call if I needed anything. He, Aunt Otelia, and Arleigh were the only family I had now. Several times I thought of calling you out in California. But I could never bring myself to do it.

The remainder of my time in Roberts I spent indoors, submerged in the emptiness of my grandmother's old house. I had a lot of time to think, although it was more like careening through a bunch of disparate memories than it was making connections between them. Nothing was very clear to me in my grandmother's house. It was the place I stored pieces of myself in the soap white, powder-scented rooms that obedient children know they are not to play in. I was left with this enervating sense of porousness, of insubstance, as if I was light enough and weak enough to float away on a tear—so I shed none. And haven't you too come to realize that each tear, shed or unshed, carries a little of us away, body and soul, bit by bit? I never attended church during those three weeks, and after Uncle Rudy left I stopped answering the phone.

Some of the older women began to stop by with food and kind words. One Saturday morning Mrs. Francine brought me breakfast—crispy fried scrapple with grits, biscuits, and scrambled eggs. (Women were always preparing food for me. I can link intervals in my adult life to a series of meals prepared by a variety of women. Is there some cultural precedent for that? Is the warmest expression of female concern to prepare and offer a meal? Or was I just the coddled bastard who in some way expected it all, as Paula would suggest when we argued?) Mrs. Francine sipped on a cup of coffee while I ate. She told me about her legs and how painful it can be to grow old. There were questions about school, fond reminiscences of "Mrs. Lydia," even a comment about you.

"There's been a lot of pain in this town this year. First that mess with the Walker boy and now your grandmother. But God only tests those he's chosen."

On the Sunday that followed, Oliver Brooks came by on his way from church. Reverend Duncan and some of the other men had asked him to offer me help with any financial matters I might have had. When I told him that my Uncle Rudy had seen to it he decided to advise me on other things.

"You know," he said, "a little bit of church ain't neva hurt nobody." He also wanted to be sure that I was going back to school. "Boy, you know how many old men round here wish they had the chance you got? You better git on back up to that school." It had always been my intention.

I saw Norris Gambrill on Monday. My grandmother had in her will that everything would go to me. She had about eight thousand dollars in savings, a small life-insurance policy, the house and property. Mr. Gambrill suggested that I rent the house and sell my grandmother's beauty shop. He said he would manage everything for 15 percent. We settled on 10. With what was left, plus my small scholarship, I could finish school comfortably. I took my last look at Roberts through the window of a Greyhound bus late that Monday evening. I've never been back.

I eventually took my rescheduled finals and, against Uncle Rudy's wishes, spent Christmas break in a cheap D.C. motel. I developed my fondness for bourbon then, and once or twice invited one of the better-looking local prostitutes to my room.

Actually what I spent most of my time doing in that motel room was reading books and watching the news on television, scanning through the paper. What times, what times. What were you doing in '65 out at Stanford? Wasn't that the year Watts burned? Did those events inspire you? Was yours the seething intellect that spurred marches and pickets? Or were you tucked away in some archaeology textbook, learning how to decipher the mystery of decaying things? I bet you did both. You'd have the mental bandwidth for both. Or perhaps you were involved until you saw that things were about to snap. It always seemed to me that after Kennedy was shot in Dallas, cynicism, apathy, and randomness began to be a more prevalent form of behavior for the white population. I guess that's not such an original thought. But for me 1965 was kind of a harbinger of everything that was going to happen. It was all right there. You could really tell that things were leading to some crowning chaos. I can't give you a list of specific events—what I recall are the sensational headlines, a general tetchiness, an impression of growing disorientation. Aside from the murders in the South and the escalating war, I remember things such as a man setting himself afire on the steps of the Pentagon, a sailor being given thirty days' hard labor for refusing to take a peace sign from his uniform.

The attitudes that belied these actions were not new ones for us. They had been engendered through the accretion of a history and an experience we were no longer willing to enjoin. We were challenging our alienness, marching, singing, refusing all the old capitulations. And I guess if it was overstated it was because it had been pent up too long, for fear of what it might elicit. (But didn't it begin that way, in the field songs some ancestors sang in their jaundiced new tongues?) There was a certain subversiveness about airing such things in the post-Birmingham sixties (now that the master understood what those work songs had been about) because it ran counter to the larger ideals of fairness, justice, and morality that other Americans had believed they as a nation exemplified. To some we became a nagging indelible stain on that claim.

Toward the end of the sixties, violence was the only thing left—I mean real violence, the moiling agitated ferment that stays just a few sentences away from combustion, the sneering rage of bricks and stones in the face of a trained and anxious white militia. Anger makes its own path, and ours could only be detoured for so long. Even if King had walked out of Memphis without a scratch, cities would still have burned.

Looking back now, it's easy to see what happened—a group of isolated shouts escalating in their collective contumacy. Remember, then, that it was within the body of that appeal that I began to think about what I would do next. I had a small source of income and enough money to finish school, my grades were fair, and I was not too concerned with being drafted. That fear of floating away is a very real memory. There was so much going on, so much to consider, so much pivoting on where the next line should be drawn.

So as you might expect things came to their own conclusion. New Year's Day 1966, I opened my eyes to see a woman staring at me from the foot of the bed. Her name was Jewel, Jewel Boston. I'd met her the night before in a liquor store on Fourteenth and I. She was a maid at the Shoreham with New Year's Eve off and a no-show date. She had bartered the night off with one of the other maids—a woman from West Virginia who knew that Jay and the Americans were booked at the hotel through New Year's and wanted to see the show.

Jewel and I ended up down on Seventh Street at the Howard Theater, where we pushed our way in to see Otis Redding perform. We danced, got drunk, kissed outside like pure white trash, and finally came back to the motel.

I remember her clearly the next morning (for she was one face of my dilemma) sitting stone-cold naked at the edge of the bed, rubbing cocoa butter onto her legs, not the least bit embarrassed, wholly confident in her deportment. With her fingertips she worked in small concentric circles from calf to thigh, her skin becoming as shiny as a polished pecan shell. The waxy-sweet smell of cocoa butter marched through the room, inescapable. It lingered in my nostrils, in my chest—hotter than the smoke of any cigarette, burning the way bourbon does on the way down. It had become her smell, now entwined in that instant for all time with my memory of "our" night.

She moved her attention to the insides of her thighs, parting her legs slightly, just enough to reach the crease of inner thigh and mons veneris. And there it was, the pussy regnant.

When she had finished with the lotion she stood up to inspect herself in the mirror. What was she looking for? She was tilting her head from side to side, deliberating on every part of her body. She would make tweaks here and there—a touch of cocoa butter to the breasts, a touch to the hips, a daub on a little ashy patch above the knee. And still, even after all that, there was just the slightest suggestion of dissatisfaction in her face as she watched herself move away from the mirror.

For some reason, at that very instant, I was struck with the weight of my own nascent dissatisfaction. The night before, I'd told myself that I could set up house in that motel room with Jewel and be the happiest man on earth. Perhaps it had been my own emptiness speaking (sometimes you have to live out a desire to know just how empty it is), or perhaps it was the inconsequence of the life I had been leading that bothered me most. I still heard my grandmother's warning, emanating like a hiss from some hole in my consciousness. To put it simply, guilt had crept into the situation. How much longer could I stay here? The spring semester would begin in two weeks and I hadn't even registered for classes.

Jewel slipped on her panties and asked me about breakfast. She wanted to know where we were going. Where indeed.

I buried my head under the covers and made a decision. Not only would I go back to school, but I would run track in the spring. That had real appeal. Yes, running seemed the thing to do. As it turned out, that would be the same semester I'd meet Paula Bond.

■ ■ ■

Look at the time, past ten already. I guess my little grandmother update ended up taking longer than I thought it would. And I haven't forgotten about Carl. It's not like I'm avoiding him or anything. It seems I often start out to tell you something and I'm led someplace entirely unexpected. I guess no memory or recollection need be linear. And I wonder if that's why things seem clearer somehow in retrospect. Perhaps in that perspective, unbound by the limits of the present, the true relationship of things is surrendered. Dr. Theodore may have even tried to tell me something like that once, but I wasn't really listening. Nothing happens in the present that wasn't begun in the past. Unfortunately, I won't have time to write much more today. Donna came in and set my clock ahead for me today and informed me that I'm scheduled for a CAT scan at eleven-fifteen this morning. And then Paula called to say that she would be making an afternoon visit. It looks like I won't have an opportunity to write more until tomorrow. Of course for you, that's only the turn of a page.

nine

Something happened today that I can't get out of my mind. (I know you're probably wondering about Carl. I haven't forgotten.) There's been another development. Paula won't be visiting me here anymore. I won't be seeing Dr. Theodore again either. After what happened yesterday, I told Donna I didn't want my wife or that Greek coming in here again. Don't ask me how she did it. I don't know what she said or what strings she pulled, but after Paula left she came in and told me that Dr. Theodore would be going away. She also told me Paula had been asked to put her weekly visits on hold.

Dr. Theodore I won't miss too much at all. What could I have told him that he would have understood? It's not like telling you. But I really hadn't intended for things to go the way they did with Paula. I love her, Paul; I do love her and I wish desperately that I could find more comfort in that now. It's just that she insists on continuing this cheerful little production about the baby and the wonderful life the three of us will have together as soon as I get well. When she started with all of that yesterday I just lost it. I told her she'd be better off getting an abortion than thinking she could build a life in this world. That baby is already labeled,

I told her. She was in tears by the time the nurses came. They had heard my ranting all the way down the hall. I shouldn't have taken it to such an extreme, I know. With my speech the way it is, Paula probably couldn't even make out most of what I said, much less understand what I meant. She still hasn't chosen to see that we can't escape the unavoidable inertia of how *we* are all thought of. I guess I have become the fatalist after all. But what's left? Nothing seems more true to me now. No matter how much we defer to prayer or material gain or African names or the borrowed memory of some ancient Nilotic culture whose true reclamation for us is impossible, we hone only an image of belonging. Aren't these all just admissions of the presence and power of what we're perceived to be? Don't we always feel down deep that when they look at us they see someone who isn't one of them, who is less than them? (Even if it's not always their perception, isn't it always ours?) In the face of that, Dr. Bond's library is really just another "Ya'sur, boss'um!" To accept that, to really give in to the truth of the feeling, is to live your life knowing how finite hope really is; you come to understand that there is a bondage more lasting than iron. And who could live believing that? I can't make Paula understand that.

But I remember a time, in what now seems like an intermission between the sieges of some dream foretelling inexorable despair, when Paula and I confronted truths. Even if we couched them in jokes and granted them only a throwaway seriousness, we still confronted them, truths as clear as the white of an eye. It was during our second year in Baltimore; everything was new, the house, our jobs, our marriage. There's such an excitement in new things. It scares us a little; we understand the personal potential for compulsion. Paula and I reveled in it.

91

It was our habit at that time to meet after work for drinks. Usually someplace downtown. There weren't a whole lot of choices then. So we became regulars at a few places—Tio Pepe's, the Chesapeake, Marconi's. We'd always make late reservations and arrive early, preferring instead to sit at the bar until a table became available. I think it was just the novelty of sitting at the bar. We were very young. I'd have a bourbon and water, no ice, and Paula would sit there at my side, her back bolt upright in her seat (almost vaunting, I'd think) sipping her vodka and tonic like a duchess. We'd talk about work, movies. We'd laugh quietly at the most inane things—the way a particular waiter walked, the hairstyle of the woman at the far table, assorted sexual innuendos. Paula would order a chicken dish, which she would barely touch, and then spend the evening with her fork meandering across the table to pick at my broiled rockfish. I'd fuss at her for not being judicious in her choice of food, but she'd still end up getting full on my dinner. In the end we'd order another bottle of wine and watch the restaurant thin out while we tried to decide what we would do next.

We'd arrive home after midnight, still giddy from all the alcohol and carousing. Paula would remember a late movie on Channel 5 that she didn't want to miss—some melodrama from the fifties that always seemed to star Susan Hayward. Invariably we'd find ourselves in the family room watching the movie play out, Paula rolling spongy pink curlers into her hair and me sipping on a bourbon. This was our time for serious discussion, a time to analyze and codify things somehow rendered incongruous by daylight and the white spaces we moved through.

One night in particular I remember the movie was *Imitation of Life*—the 1959 version with Lana Turner, John

Gavin, Sandra Dee, Juanita Moore, and Susan Kohner as Sarah Jane, the black girl who wanted to be white.

It surprised me to discover in later years that this movie held no special significance for whites, if it was even remembered at all. You know as well as I, that for any black person over thirty-five, *Imitation of Life* has an enduring celebrity—what advertisers would term an 85 percent recognition index among blacks over thirty-five years of age. I guess it's not hard to explain. It was more than just another late fifties melodrama. It seems cartoonish now; the then-touted bold and realistic plot is embarrassingly fraught with the popular racism of the time. But what we remember and still see, perhaps, was the novelty of black actors in integral supporting roles, a whole subplot spun through the lives of an otherwise all-white cast. This alone would have been enough to raise endearing emotional tides (we're no less stupidly sentimental than anyone else). But since the film also presented the prodigal daughter motif, and a teary funeral scene—all with the verisimilitude that passes for Hollywood social consciousness—its easy communal truths became a powerful confirmation of what we already knew.

I remember the first time it was aired on television. It was a big event for us in Roberts. Remember, it turned out to be quite a night. We must have been, what, fourteen or fifteen, I don't know. I remember most of us were making plans to be near a TV that night. I remember hearing the girls talk about it between class saying, "Oh, y'all know what's comin' on t'night, don't chu?"

Nisey Brooks had invited me to her house to watch the movie with her. It was the closest thing to a date she was allowed. Her father, Oliver, was the first black in Roberts to own a color TV. The story went that he had purchased it from a skinny white man in a beat-up Nash Rambler. No one had ever seen the man before. He went door to door, to every house in the neighborhood, trying to sell the set to anyone brave enough to buy it. The Brooks home had been the last stop. After word got around about the purchase, people began to speak of Oliver Brooks as a shrewd man, someone to consult on business dealings.

When you found out that Crystal Merritt would also be at Nisey's, you decided to tag along with me, knowing that even though you weren't invited, no one would object to Paul Walker's company. Back then you were the little black prophet with the word from God. (I always wondered how you knew Crystal would be there, or if you really even expected her to be there. I know you said she told you, but you seemed a little too surprised when we arrived and saw her sitting in the kitchen.)

Everyone cried at the end of the movie, although you and I tried hard to keep it back. But the real event occurred when the Brookses went upstairs to bed. Mr. Brooks let us know that we should be making our way home soon. Before we did, you managed to turn out the lights, and we had the girls alone for fifteen minutes. It was the first time I had my balls fondled. It must have also been Nisey's first time as a fondler, too. She was a little too rough. I walked out of there half doubled over with cramps.

I made the mistake of recounting the whole event to Paula in slightly exaggerated detail as we watched the movie. I had thought she hadn't heard me, focused as she was on John Gavin stealing a kiss from Lana Turner. But when the scene dissolved, she wanted to know more about Nisey Brooks. I told her my involvement with Nisey hadn't amounted to much and that I hadn't seen her since I left Roberts.

She had other questions, each more piercing. It was only fair, I suppose. We had already discussed our old loves long ago and now here I was taunting her with one I'd left out. I was helped by a tense moment in the movie, the scene where Troy Donahue beats the daylights out of Sarah Jane after discovering that her mother was a "nigger." We coiled and recoiled with every blow. Our disgust was still very visceral after all that time. A conditioned response? I called us Pavlov's Negroes and Paula laughed, twisting another curler into her hair. As she did, I saw one of her breasts slide out from her nightgown. She has nice breasts, pert and full, but not grotesquely massive in any sense. They command attention. Or maybe it's her nipples that do. They're so distinctively large, dark, and thick—like a section of a Tootsie Roll.

She had stopped laughing; Sarah Jane was pulling herself up from the street.

"You know," Paula said, still fiddling with a curler, "that girl reminds me of someone."

"Nisey? You never met her."

"No, not Nisey. We'll get back to Nisey. I meant Sarah Jane there."

"Let's see, you'll say she's like Karen Glenn from your office, right?"

"Karen Glenn? No! Karen's a floozy, but she wouldn't mess with any white boys and she knows she's black. I was thinking more in the family, like...Lydia Ware Covington."

"Here we go. The my-grandmother-was-a-bitch thesis. You never even met her, Pau—"

"You've given me enough to go on. Besides, I know her type." She was trying to vex me now. My grandmother was a subject that she knew she could easily work under my skin.

"Type, huh? Tell me something. Do nipples sting just a little when they get hard?" She was confused by the statement until she looked down and saw her exposed breast. Smiling, half attempting to act coy, she pulled the nightgown away from her shoulder, giving me a full unobstructed view.

"There is a type," she said nonchalantly, the Virginia in her voice more noticeable. "There were women in Richmond who my father said tried to pass for white when he was a boy."

"Well I guess anything 'yo daddy' says must be true. And my grandmother never tried to pass for wh—"

"I'm sure your grandmother had a bigger influence on you than my daddy had on me." She spoke quickly—a kind of hit-and-run technique—smiling, her head slightly bent, rolling one last curler up along the bottom of her hairline. "I think you're trying to change the subject. Didn't you sit right on that couch once and tell me yourself that your grandmother tried to pass for white?" She let the top of the gown slip to her waist. I removed my pants. We were playing a game, tease and fuck—a game of control. The object was to see who would grab whom first. She spoke before I could reply. "You know it, Billy, your grandmother would have approved of me even if I were an evil bitch from hell. Just as long as I was light skinned, right?"

"Paula, you never even met her! How can you know something about someone you've never even met? Or are women from Virginia just routinely jealous of dead people? And I never sai—" She kept interrupting me, trying to speak at the exact instant I did. "I never sa...I never said ...I never said she tried to pass for white and you know it! You're just jealous of her because she was such a giving person." None of it was working on her. She just laughed at everything I aimed her way.

"Giving? What did she give you? She gave you a roof and meals. You were her only son's only child. She wasn't going to abandon you. And that's not the point anyway. You're still trying to change the subject 'cause you know what I said about her is true. You told me the story yourself, Billy; you told me yourself and don't sit there looking all surprised either! That story about the pictures. It's true; I'm not making it up! Tell me again."

When I was around eight or nine, I had come across a box of old photographs while exploring in my grandmother's attic. This was almost two years after the fire, and although I was living with my grandmother then, I still half expected my parents to come for me; expected it if only as a daydream or one of those eerie surreal fantasies children sometimes have at night once they have been tucked in and left alone in the darkness to fall asleep.

The photos I found were old, cardboard mounted and peeling with age. The people in them were stranger still—a bunch of austere faces in their Sunday best. But there was another quality in those fading sepia countenances—something imperious and grave. I knew I had made a find, like a scholar who stumbles upon the missing pictographs from some ancient bowdlerized history.

That afternoon my grandmother and I went through every photo in that box. I'd pick one out and she'd give me a name (if remembered) and a little history of the subject's life—the more tragic and ironic of which I'd commit to memory like a new word. Perhaps in this way we learn to sound the present with the past.

One of the photos we came across was a shot of my

grandmother as a child, sitting on the lap of a gaunt woman. She told me the woman was her mother. (I remember how strange that seemed to me. I'd never considered that someone as old as my grandmother would have pictures of her parents.) She took the photo from me and held it quietly for a long heavy moment. I think she had forgotten it even existed. It was spotted with water stains, giving it a blotchy sallow hue, like the worn bone handle of an old knife. She moved the photo closer to her face as if expecting its captive figures to breathe with life. It was one of those instances when time seems to linger in the effusiveness of the moment. She kissed the photo and then began to fan herself with it, slowly, pulling me closer as she did.

"My ole momma was black as tar," she said, "but you know, I luved her anyways." In her voice was that fading echo quality of a call coming through on a bad long-distance connection.

"That's what she gave you!" Paula said, knowing I wouldn't retell the story to her. "Even though her mother, her own mother, didn't look like some white bitch, she still loved her! Anything about us that doesn't look close to white is . . . embarrassing!"

"How can you even—"

"Better to have 'good hair' and a little poin—"

"Paula, you can't just lump—"

"A little pointed Scarlett O'Hara nose! And Lord help you if you weren't light skinned, because the lighter your skin, the better. It all gets passed on."

"You can't just lump my grandmother in with every old black person you know. It's not fair."

"It's not just old ones! There were guys in college who only went out with me because I'm light skinned! One of them actually told me that he had a lunch-bag test; if a girl was darker than a lunch bag he didn't go out with her! He actually told me that—like I should be honored or something!" She stopped abruptly, realizing, I think, that she'd strayed from the intent of the game. She put things back on track by cupping her breasts in her hands and pointing them at me.

"Of course," she said, "these might have had something to do with those dates too. What do you think; better than Nisey's little sore titties?" She hefted each slightly as if daring me to guess their weight. What gorgeous nipples she has. Breasts have no erotic value for me if I can't see nipples.

But my part in the game was to resist. So I continued, knowing now that I had made her lose control despite herself. I had a defense now. I also shifted my position so that my growing erection would be easily visible. Then I said, in a slow studied tone, "We're talking about beauty, what looks beautiful, and everyone thinks they know something about that."

"Yep, there's certainly no consensus on beauty," she came back, pointing a breast at me for emphasis. (She'd had a lot of vodka.) "Like these, they're beautiful, don't you think?"

"Now I'm sure," I continued in my impenetrable charade, "that you got fed a lot of contempt by darker sisters when you were growing up. This whole skin-color thing is depressing, isn't it? We've been fed—"

"You can feed on these," she said, pinching her nipples this time. "Ah come on; baby want a little titty? Mama's baby want a little titty? Come get a little tit—"

"We've been fed on someone else's standards of beauty for so long. All that matters now is how close to them you look."

"Yep, we've strayed from the bosom of the motherland. Now come on home to Mama's ti—"

"No black person in America would say they wanted

knottier hair or thicker lips or a broader nose. I guess the goal for black women in America is to look like Lena Horne or Dorothy Dandridge. Any 'American' will tell you that those are pretty sisters. And you know what the irony of it all is? White people are more confused than we are."

"That's right, miscegenation in America is something that they started, honey!" she said. I had breached the wall and she realized it instantly. She began to laugh. With her curlers and bared bosom, she looked like the model for some postmodern fertility fetish. She took my drink from the coffee table and swallowed it in one gulp, as if to say, Well take that! And then after it had gone down, "Owww! God, Billy, how can you drink that stuff?"

And then she looked at me and we both began to laugh— she, as if the absurdity of what we had been doing had just struck her. She couldn't stop laughing, trying to remove her nightgown completely as the intensity of the laughter grew, trying to pull the gown over her head and finding it doubly difficult what with all the vodka she'd had. I began to nuzzle her thighs, tickling her, and through her shuddering laughter, her head half covered by the gown and her elbow caught in a sleeve, she said "Billy, wait . . . Billy!" and then giving into the laughter again "Bil-ly . . . you know, I don't even think I'm ovulating now!" And finally with the gown off and me pulling her closer, I remember her saying, "You know, Lena and Dorothy *are* beautiful women." I agreed.

ten

I made an admission to myself this morning. It's taken me some time to gather the resolve, and having done so I'm now left wondering if perhaps Dr. Bond had been right after all. Perhaps there is some courage in reserve somewhere.

What I am now able to admit is that for the last two days I've avoided telling you about Carl Rice. I'm sure you'd figured as much on your own. I'd like to believe that acknowledging my fear portends the eventual completion of this journal, since I have sometimes doubted my willingness to relive it all over again. Dr. Theodore once told me that during therapy, as people get close to their "issues" they often become evasive. I'm sure he said that as an attempt to coax me into talking more—which I wouldn't do. But he was right. Carl is, I suppose, at the heart of all my "issues." That being the case, you might think that I'd know him as well as myself. Yet Carl Rice was more unknowable than anyone I'd ever met, as if he were merely a shadow cast by some smoldering expectation.

He has the body of a sprinter. In fact, that's the most lasting impression I have of Carl—the aging athlete. He moves like a sprinter. There's this curious precision in his walk. Perhaps the swagger of an aging man who knows he still looks good. It always reminded me of the way Ali would walk into the ring toward the end of his career, before the brain damage became apparent.

We were both born in September, Carl on the twentieth—two days and two years behind me. And so we share a house of sorts, if you follow the stars. (Donna tells me that such things are important.) Most of the time, I was never sure where I stood with him. Once, after he had tried unsuccessfully to persuade me to join in the condemnation of the company's hiring practices, he angrily called me a "house nigger." On other occasions I had been an "Oreo," and once a "lackey." (A running argument at that time was over African names—Carl was considering one for himself.) Still, at other times we spoke with that casual familiarity black people share among themselves. He would compliment me on knowing how to "play the game" or kid me about what a "corporate brother" I had become. I can't really say we were friends, though.

Our relationship was in some ways a matter of proximity. There was this terminal awareness of each other's presence. In a business unit of twenty-eight hundred, Carl and I were two of four black managers. We also had the added distinction of having similar high-visibility positions. We ended up working together a lot. At a distance people would sometimes even mistake us for each other. He's also tall, and he shares my affinity for Italian clothes— the Ungaro suits, Armani ties. But of course for Carl it's more than that. He explained to me once how our style of dress is suited for the executive who does not (or cannot) truly aspire to the "pin-striped anonymity of the status quo."

There are other things you should know about Carl, a few telling foibles of the proud brother. He has a fourteen-year-old daughter named Kenya and a twelve-year-old son named Haim, both by his ex-wife, the daughter of an orthodox Jewish printer from New Jersey. Yes, Carl Rice had crossed the color line! I always told myself that one day I would confront Carl with this incongruity. But after the divorce, it didn't seem appropriate. The children now live in California with their mother, the former Marcia Siegel, in a comfortable apartment in West Hollywood. Carl and Marcia have been divorced for six years now. I've never been told just what happened. Carl never let on that they were having problems until the very end. I remember asking him how Marcia's parents had felt about the marriage from the beginning. All he said was, "Well, it wasn't no synagogue wedding." Marcia now works as a publicist for MGM Studios. In Baltimore, she taught contemporary fiction at Goucher College.

They met at NYU, where Carl had gone after being booted out of Howard University. He had protested what he thought was the then elitist mock-white curriculum of the school, by occupying the dean's office in whiteface and a three-piece suit.

Maybe the most important thing you should know is that while I was liked and generally respected at Varitech, Carl was tolerated. The topic, no doubt, of many a hushed discussion. During a meeting I'd heard Len Townes once call him an agitator. (I think he forgot I was there, for as soon as he made his comment and saw me sitting at the back of the room he quickly added a few words about the great job Carl was doing in graphic arts.) Carl is perhaps what a lot of whites would describe, artlessly, as a militant. In truth, though, he had the same fervent views on the failings of the social and corporate worlds of white America that many blacks shared. Only he made no effort to conceal these views whenever the subject arose, although he never invited such discourse. I refused to discuss such things in the plant, but Carl and I would often talk off-site. What had really given Carl his reputation was his well-publicized dissatisfaction with the company's hiring practices. In the end I think it was only the fear of litigation that kept him employed. He was ultimately dispatched to a position of visibility with no chance of advancement. The details of his particular exile are lurid and numerous, but why go into that? You'd never get your question answered, and besides, I've procrastinated enough.

Now, I think I *had* told you a little about Carl two days ago. Let's see, where had I left you? Oh yes, I had started to tell you about the afternoon I confronted Carl with the CPT fliers. Do you remember? I found myself standing in his office with one of the damned things in my hand. Did I tell you he had known about them all along? Before he even opened his mouth, I knew that. It was the way he looked up at me when I laid the sheet on his desk. He beamed with his old self-satisfied smirk.

"I had expected you to call me as soon as you saw one of those," he said. I told him I hadn't understood the message. He just shook his head. "You knew what CPT meant. That should have told you right off."

Things came back then, in color and sound. The voices first. My grandmother's voice, laughing with Mrs. Francine after church one Sunday.

"Lawd, here they go agin talkin' 'bout choir practice, startin' promptly mind ju, at sebum o'clock. They mean sebum o'clock CPT. I ain't neva seen these Nigros here started nothin' on time."

And there was something I heard your mother say one

morning as I waited for you to leave for school.

"Paul, you betta step it up. School don't run on colored people's time."

When the voices toggled off, I was aware of just what I had forgotten. How many years had I not known? I couldn't decide. It was such a requisite thing, a little cultural joke among ourselves. I stood there wondering when it was that I had stopped remembering.

"It's mainly a bulletin," he said. "We want to make sure everybody comes to the meetings. Man, how could you forget CPT? I just don't under—"

"What meetings?"

"Billy, you do work here, don't you? Haven't you been following what's going on? But you don't get out in the shop much, do you? You have to stay close to Mr. Haviland and that nitwit Lloyd Harrow."

"I work for Haviland and I work with Lloyd," I flared. "Why should I be in the shop?"

"Tell me, Billy," Carl asked, "what work does Lloyd Harrow do? There's no job description for his position. He's been down here almost every day this week, wasting my time with his bullshit. You know what he wanted to talk about today? How he believes that Jimi Hendrix was killed by the CIA for playing 'The Star-Spangled Banner' like he did at Woodstock. Says his father has a friend who knows for sure. Can you believe that? Everybody knows it was the FBI that did it."

"The fliers, Carl, what about the fliers?"

"Haven't you heard anything?"

"Believe it or not, my own problems require most of my attention."

"Well the rumors have been rolling around here for the last month. I'm surprised Haviland or your boy Lloyd hasn't asked you about it."

He was about to continue, but someone entered the room. A young man I was sure I recognized, but I couldn't recall from where. Carl greeted him casually, introducing me only as "a brother from executive row."

"Yeah, I seen you around," he responded.

His name was Everett Peale and I had seen him, I suddenly remembered, in the cafeteria. He was one of the people in the kitchen. I'd seen him serving food at the steam tables. But he had another job. As Carl explained, Everett was responsible for distributing the CPT fliers around the shop floor. He had in fact come to Carl for more fliers. Carl took out his desk keys and opened the last drawer on the bottom left side. As he did, Everett turned to me.

"So," he said, "we gonna see you at Fridee's meetin'?"

Before I could answer, Carl quickly interrupted, handing over a stack of fliers as he did.

"He'll be there. Look, you better get out of here before you're seen. And remember, put those up in the morning before six and only in the shop. We don't want to spill this until we're ready."

When he left, Carl poured himself a cup of coffee and lit another Salem. I sat down beside his desk. I couldn't help feeling that Carl had set me up, because now I was involved.

"That boy," Carl said, taking a drag from the cigarette. "I swear, I don't know about him. You know the CPT See Quarter Till thing was all his idea. I had to bite my tongue over that one."

"You lost me, Carl. What do you mean bite your tongue, why?"

"The CPT part was probably a good idea—no white person knows what that means—but the See Quarter Till stuff...I hate to hear us talking like that in this day and age." I still didn't know what he was talking about and he must have seen it in my face.

"The fliers," Carl went on, "are a good way to let everyone know when we're meeting. See, we can't be too open about announcing meeting times and places, because that will tip the hat. So what we do is post the fliers when we're going to meet. That way everyone knows we're going to meet, but not when or where. Now, to let everyone know that, we have one person everyone can go to for specific times and places. That person is supposed to be different each time, but this machinist named Earl Gaines has pretty much ended up with the job. I wanted to use a code name or something for Earl, so no one reading the fliers will know who he is. At one of the early meetings, Everett says why don't we use Earl's nickname, Quarter Till. They all thought it was funny. There was nothing I could do."

"Quarter Till?" I said. "So what's that supposed to mean?"

"They call him that because they say he's blacker than quarter to midnight—get it?" He shook his head. "What do you think white people think when they hear us saying things like that? It just saves them from making the insult." He shook his head again. I sometimes believe that Carl cultivated his image with as much care as I did. He pandered to them more than he wanted to admit. He was the angry black man they anticipated.

Having now finished the cigarette, he took a Hershey's bar from his desk, which he ate like a Danish along with the coffee. He still hadn't told me what was going on. What were the fliers and meetings for?

"There's going to be some trouble, Billy. Big trouble. All the brothers in the machinist's union want to walk."

"Walk? From the union, or from the company?"

"Both! A few months ago the union got wind of the new plant the company's building in Mexico. I'm not even going to ask you if you knew about it. But when the union found out, Jack Dulaney goes up to Haviland's office and apparently after a few days of discussion they made a deal. I don't know the specifics of what was said. The bottom line is we got shortchanged. There were some guarantees made about what jobs would be secure and how that would be decided. It's a flat seniority scam, which leaves us high and dry. When the union made the announcement a couple of brothers even went to Dulaney. Here they thought the union was representing their best interests and they get screwed. To top it off all Dulaney does is go into this song and dance about how this deal will be good for everybody. I've dealt with that Irish son of a bitch before. Man, those people are the biggest racists around—you ever notice how many of them belong to these ultra-right-wing political groups? It's them and the Mormons. Now those people, the only thing they want to see black is nightfall. Who is that one glassy-eyed saltine from Utah? I saw him on—"

"Carl, Carl; are you telling me there's going to be a strike?"

"I'm telling you that every black machinist at this company is going to get real loud, real soon. They want to split off from the union, and they want to strike."

Lord, how I wanted to grab Carl and shake him silly. It was such a niggerish mess he'd gotten himself into. I wanted no part of it.

"Who is orchestrating all of this? You? Man, I hope it's not you! They could get rid of you for that. The little piece of a career you have left would be shot."

"Is that concern I hear, Billy? Don't worry, I'm just

helping out. You know, supporting my people. All I do is make copies of the fliers and attend the meetings."

"Yeah, so who runs the meetings?"

"You're not collecting information for da massa are you?" He was only half kidding.

"You just laid a lot of shit in my lap, Carl. I want to understand what's going on."

"I guess I'm just overwhelmed by all this concern. I remember last year when the black professionals' association wanted to put together that letter to Haviland decrying this company's piss-poor record of promoting blacks you didn't want any part of it. Is that the same Billy Covington who wants to know what's going on?"

"You're damned right I didn't want any part of it! It wasn't the association that put that letter together. It was you and Curt Reed. And where is he now? He had to leave the company after being stuck in some dead-end job in planning. Your letter did his career a lot of good!"

"That's only because we didn't stick together. There was no show of strength."

"That's because there was no strength in writing that letter. How can you work in a corporation as long as you have and not understand that? It's like changing your name, Carl, it's not going to change anything."

"I'm not even going to get into that with you again. But are you denying that there's a different hiring system for *us*? The system here is not fair, Billy! There are whites in management who don't even have college degrees. They have a job because some white man likes them. They fuck up; they make mistakes—everybody knows we lost that contract with IBM because Jerry Flynn mismanaged the whole project. He had no experience in what he was doing, hadn't even worked on a major winning project since he came to the company, but what do they do? They promote him to contract-development manager under Howie Frost. None of *us* would ever get that kind of break. They'll scrutinize your every credential and still pass you over! And look, they get their children hired in here, their friends, in jobs that don't even get advertised unless they're already filled. And then they complain about affirmative action! And if you have the temerity to mention how racist it all is, they look at you and say, 'Racism? Where, I don't see any? Prove it.' And of course you can never prove it because they control the information! There's always enough of them to form a consensus on anything they want to disbelieve, regardless of fact. I don't understand how you can look at that and not get mad!"

"I don't understand how you can stay in the same job for five years without any real promotion! I don't understand how you can work in a place where you have no credibility. Don't you think that some of these white boys are pissed off too because they got passed over for Flynn? And I'll tell you something else, Carl, if I had a kid you'd best believe I'd get him in here—the same way they do! And the difference between me and you, Carl, is that I could get it done. They'd do it for me. They own the system, Carl! They made it all up just for them; we weren't even a consideration. Can't you see that? You can only work in it! So I don't get into arguments with Len Townes about how sick I think the Elvis cult is and how he wasn't the king of anything, how all he did was rip off a lot of black music and mannerisms and repackage it like it was all his idea. It might have made you feel better to say all that stuff but all it does is piss people off. They don't want to have to know how you feel."

The argument I referred to took place last year in the AV

room, where Len, Carl, and I were reviewing slides for a presentation on company operations that Len was to give to an investor review board. Len came as close as I'd ever seen him to losing his facade of control, for he truly loves Elvis.

"Billy, what is this problem you have about pissing white people off?"

We both just sat there, silent, having exhausted the limits of what we could say. A truce. Then Carl took another Hershey's bar from his desk drawer. He offered me a piece, and when I declined he took a big bite. I don't understand how anyone who eats as much junk food as Carl does manages to stay so slim.

We didn't say anything else about unions, fliers, or strikes. We talked around it; we talked about the sales meeting coming up in two weeks, about the wonderful job Meeting Planners (the company I had hired to set the conference up) was doing. I told Carl I'd never been to Atlanta. He was from Athens, Georgia, and had been to Atlanta many times to visit family. For him it was a city that offered no mystery. He showed me the bluelines I'd originally come to see. It would be a nice piece when printed. Carl was a good writer, and while not a graphic artist, he had a fine aesthetic sense.

After I'd approved the bluelines and discussed the print schedule, I left—but not before Carl reminded me again of the Friday meeting. More than anything I was scared, scared that events would overtake me and that I would find no safe haven.

■ ■ ■

When I got home that day, Paula was asleep. She hadn't even heard me enter the house and awoke only at the creaking of the closet door as I hung up my clothes.

"Oh, Billy." Her head popped up, creased and damp from the pillow. "I just lay down for a second and I was out. You could have been a burglar and I wouldn't have even heard you come in. I was dreaming."

"Sex dreams, right?"

"Are you going to be nasty again today?"

"But you only have sex dreams at certain times of the month."

"And under certain conditions!" she snapped, with an angry finality that was intended to shut me up.

"How about under duress?" I asked.

She got up and went downstairs. I followed, after a trip to the bathroom. I found her in the kitchen tossing a salad at the counter. The table was set.

"Is that chicken I smell?" I said, opening the oven. I really didn't expect her to answer at this point. These rhetorical exercises of mine were more a ritual of redemption than anything else. So I continued. "You knows I's just loves me some chickin. Is dere watermelin fo' dessert?" No response.

She quietly brought the food to the table: first the salad, then the chicken, and finally a pitcher of iced tea from the refrigerator. She broke her silence when she blessed the meal.

"So," I said, taking a breast from the platter, "how was your day today?"

"So," she said, amplifying my own sarcasm, "are we actually going to talk about something now?"

"Sure, I want to talk."

She poured some iced tea into her glass and took a slow deliberate swallow. "What did the doctor tell you, Billy?"

"He told me, he told me to buy my wife a vibrator." I

don't even know why I said that. It was childish and pointless and did not go unanswered.

She let her fork drop to the plate. She may have even given it some help on the way down for it rang like a brass bell. She got up from the table and glared down at me, her eyes welling up.

Lying in this hospital bed now, I can't believe that I affixed so much of my self-esteem to something as fragile as an erection. It doesn't seem very important now.

"I can't take this shit anymore, Billy! I've got to get out of here. I'm going to stay with Karen tonight." Her voice was wobbling, she was shaking. "I'm going upstairs to pack a few things and I'm leaving."

"You're going to leave? Why? Karen going to fix you up with one of her men friends?"

"You common dog! That's probably what you think too. I'm leaving because I can't take shit like that from you anymore!"

"Can't take any more shit like what?"

"I never know how you're going to be. What I should say. Every question's the wrong question. You act like you're mad at me."

When she confronts me with the undeniable truth of my actions, there is always this stranded immutable silence, dangling opaque and viscous with wasted possibility like a drop of semen at the head of a limp cock.

"What's left for me to do, Paula? I mean what can I do? You don't know what it's like. What it does to, to think about yourself this way." I heard myself say those words and it still didn't register completely that they were coming from my lips. I had never put it in words before, laid it there naked for her, and me, to confront. It was embarrassing, scary; I felt belittled in some way. And perhaps that's what I feared most about the truth. It reduces us to the graceless raw childishness of our emotions, stripping away all the artifices of stealth we so cunningly accumulate over the years. I sat there staring at the wall.

She walked over and put her hands on my shoulders, lightly. My first impulse was to flinch away—I wasn't in need of sympathy, so I told myself. (Actually, I scarcely realized how much in need I was.) I allowed myself to be touched. Just her hands felt good. So much reassurance in a touch. It was what I needed, what I wanted always, but could never ask for directly. You have to say the words first and that's always the hardest thing to do.

"You could try to talk to me, Billy," she said. "We used to talk, remember? You walk around here most of the time like I don't exist, until you have to confront . . . it. Then you get cruel and sarcastic. Today, you saw the doctor. Before, you got like this when you talked to Arleigh. It's got to stop." She looked me in the face. "I'm the one who loves you, okay? I can't take much more of this, Billy. We don't go out anymore; we don't talk; we don't anything. I want us to try to enjoy ourselves again."

She didn't end up leaving that night. But that wasn't a guarantee that we would talk about anything that mattered. We sat before the television, watching "M*A*S*H" reruns on Channel 45, punctuating the commercials with our brief modular conversations. We turned in after the news. The last thing I heard before I dozed off was Paula saying, "I wonder why they never did much with Spearchucker in the series? They just kind of let him fade away. You know in the book, and even in the movie, he had a much bigger part . . . I love you, Billy, I really do."

eleven

There were a few more things I wanted to ask Carl when I got into work that next morning. He had avoided my questions about who was organizing things for the black workers. Nothing happens without organization, and I didn't really believe that Carl was only photocopying fliers. Calling him would be item two on my Now Remember pad. Item one was John Haviland's staff meeting. It was held every Tuesday morning at nine o'clock in John's conference room. I despised those meetings. They were so blatantly mercenary. Everyone would try so hard to look efficient in Haviland's eyes—usually at someone else's expense. The whole meeting would turn into a kind of showcase for Machiavellian advocacy. I think that's what bothered me most: all the maneuvering and duplicity was so covert. There would be joking, laughter, and concern—all the trappings of esprit de corps. But it was all tactical.

Haviland would insist that a pot of gourmet coffee be on hand—some weird blend of African and Jamaican beans. He would also have a box of his boyhood favorite, glazed cinnamon buns from Dunkin' Donuts, in the center of the conference table. Len Townes would be there, Lloyd, Neil Rosen, Howie Frost, and me.

Haviland would always be the last to arrive. While we waited for him. Len made a joke about Kaname Takahashi, the new Japanese head R&D scientist the company had just hired.

"It certainly puts a new *slant* on our business," he said. Everyone laughed. Then he made his usual Len remark, taking the largest bun from the box and saying, "It's manifest destiny."

John Haviland had his own style of entering the room—any room, actually. As usual, he came in hurried, ruddy-faced and unsmiling, full of this radiant urgency. The rest of us were impelled to attention. I guess that's what power is all about.

So things had begun routinely enough. John gave his usual summary of last week's triumphs and screwups. He talked about sales, revenues, the flatness of our stock, making more of a push to the investor community, and progress on the construction of the Mexico facility. (Yes, I had lied to Carl.) Next, each of us updated him on work in our areas. Everyone was called on in turn to speak, except Lloyd, whose job it was to take the minutes. Topics were identified as needing further discussion, things like distributor margins on one of our product lines, pricing issues on the new wave solder, third-quarter forecasts and bookings. Sometimes there would be disagreements. Haviland never took sides, but kept the discussions focused. His favorite tactic was to say things like "Flesh it out for me" or "Substantiate that."

My turn to speak came. I was usually last, so I tended to talk fast. I'd hired a company out of North Carolina called Meeting Planners to handle the majority of this year's sales

conference. Haviland wanted to know how that was working out, as we were a week away from the conference. I
explained how they had taken care of most of the room
reservations, banquets, and staging for the presentation
night.

"My group was only minimally involved this year," I
said.

"I hope you're more involved than that," Haviland said,
wanting to know more.

The instant Len began to ask questions too, I knew the
little covert war of words had begun. "Have we worked with
these people before, Bill?" he asked. "You've been keeping
an eye on them, I guess?"

"He raises a good point there, Bill," Neil Rosen added.
"Didn't you have some unexpected problems with that 8A
firm you hired last year, Len? I forget their name, but they
were suppose to do the software integration for that auto-
mated facility in White Plains. That was a disaster, as I
remember."

"Yes, that's right," Len said, so very composed. "That's
exactly why I raised the point I did."

"Hey, how much did that end up costing us?" Howie said
to Neil. "Didn't you put, what's her name . . . Mary Meigs
out in White Plains to try to contain costs on that? I never
got the final figure. I understand it cost—"

"It cost too much," Haviland interrupted. "That's one
we fucked up on. We can't afford too many more of those,
especially with the way sales are looking this quarter."

Haviland instructed me to move on, so I talked about the
most pressing projects my group was handling, some direct
mail, the new ad campaign. When I finished, Haviland
closed his folder. This is usually the signal that the meeting
is over. We all stood to leave.

"One more thing," Haviland said. It caught everyone by surprise. "Has anybody else seen one of these things around?"

From the breast pocket of his coat, he produced a single piece of paper, folded lengthwise. He opened it up and laid it on the table for us to inspect. It was one of Carl's fliers. CPT See Quarter Till had made it to the executive conference room.

We all hovered over the conference table, examining the piece of paper as if it were some bizarre dead animal. I kept my mouth shut. No one else had seen the flier before except Len (of course) who thought he'd seen one in manufacturing somewhere.

"That's where I found this one, in manufacturing," Haviland said. "I saw a kid taping it to the wall."

"And he wouldn't tell you what it was for?" Neil Rosen asked.

"He ran when he saw me."

The room suddenly got very, very still.

"Is this something we should look into, John?" Len said earnestly.

"I don't know what this thing is," he said, holding the flier up for emphasis. When Haviland gets demonstrative it's trouble. I kept my lips tightly together.

"If it were out in my shop, why didn't it come through HR?" Len said incredulously.

"That's a good question, Len, so I can assume that you don't know what it is either," Haviland said. "It's not about bowling, or a fishing tournament. None of the floor managers in your area," he pointed to Len for emphasis, "knew anything about it—I've already had Lloyd check that out. Maybe it's nothing. Maybe it's not. Right now I'm concerned until I find out for sure either way. We just came through a tricky negotiation with the union; Mexico's coming on-line. I don't want any problems." He put the flier into his folder and closed it. The meeting had ended.

"I'll look into it," Len volunteered, still flush faced from Haviland's inference that things were happening in Len's area that he knew nothing about.

I left the meeting with this creeping sense of dread. I was again wishing that Carl had never told me anything. Haviland had been hedging. He obviously had some larger misgivings about the flier that he hadn't addressed directly. I was also bothered that Lloyd hadn't mentioned anything earlier about the fliers. It wasn't like him not to tell me what he had been up to. In fact, Lloyd seemed to slip away right after the meeting.

I guess that for everyone who lives between the white spaces paranoia is almost the proxy of one's concern. Perhaps as a group *we* take our bearings through a collective suspicion, through a kind of enduring unglamorous vigil. Like CPT, this is something else I'd forgotten.

On the way back to my office, I began to assemble theories. Suppose, I asked myself, that Haviland knew what the fliers were about. Suppose he only brought it up in the meeting to see if I would volunteer any information. Perhaps it was my last chance to solidify my allegiance before the hammer came down. If it was indeed a test, I'd failed. I wasn't even sure why.

Nancy was waiting for me when I returned. Haviland's office had just called, she told me. He wanted to see me right away. I lost my breath for a second. It had to be about the fliers; what else could it be? I would tell him everything I knew. I'd bargained with my fear for this course of action. But even before I came to his office, I knew I wouldn't say anything.

When I entered the anteroom, Claire Watson smiled up at me from her desk. She informed me that Haviland was speaking to Len Townes behind closed doors.

"I'm sure he'll be free in a minute," she said. "I know he really wants to talk to you."

Apparently Len had popped in with something burning to discuss. My mind raced between supposition and whatever truth I could find in my situation. What did I know for certain? More than I cared to, I decided. What did Haviland know? What should I let him know?

I began my ritual of polite empty chatter with Claire. It's a tribute we all learn to pay to the secretaries of powerful men. I truly liked Claire, though, so there wasn't much pain involved in the effort.

Len left Haviland's office without too much fanfare. The door opened and he walked out. There wasn't the usual lingering conversation.

"Hello again," Haviland said in a calm friendly tone. "Come on in why don't you." He closed the door behind us, motioning me to the conference table I'd left just a few moments before. When I sat down, he said, "Hey, that's the same seat Townes was in. You better check the legs." We both laughed. "So, I haven't talked to you in a while," he continued, "but I see you're still sporting around in that Jaguar, so I guess things are going okay for you. How's Paula?" He smiled.

I told him all was well, but I knew I was not expected to make conversation. We had already gone about as far off task as Haviland ever let himself get these days. All the homey, very calculated palaver was just that.

But our conversations hadn't always been so perfunctory. As I told you, early in my career we'd worked together often. I'd come to like John, admire him even. Despite his devouring ambition, I found that he had unusual interests for an executive. He read books. Not the usual business-trend, management-technique stuff, I mean real literature. *Village Voice* stuff. At heart, I think he was still a beatnik. That was his era. He had come back from Korea, wandered across the country, and finally ended up in New York, where he finished his degree. To a boy raised in the coal-fields of western Pennsylvania, New York in the early fifties must have seemed the center of the universe. He immersed himself in the Village scene. He told me once that he'd drunk beer with Jack Kerouac (I had trouble believing that one) and once stood no less than two feet away from Miles Dewey Davis himself. In fact, he had every record Miles ever made and had seen him play on occasions too numer-ous to count. (I know of at least one business trip to California—ostensibly to explore a distributor channel for our products in the Pacific rim—that was scheduled around a Miles concert in Berkeley.)

But that was the old Haviland. His crack about Len Townes had been an allusion, of sorts, to that man. Not that we were ever great chums, but he was accessible in the old days and I had come to know something of that man. I didn't really know much at all about the CEO John Havi-land, with his swept-back mane of graying hair and his ceramic blue eyes. He was still the one person at Varitech most responsible for my career. But I didn't know if he still regularly read the book section of the *Village Voice*, or what he thought of the "new" Miles. All I really had to go on was that comment he'd made that day in the Jaguar ("if you only talk about what you know, and all you talk about is work, then you've got a problem"). That was about as much as I knew about him now—that, and the fact that the John Haviland seated across the table from me that day, poised to speak, was making me nervous.

"My mother used to say she could feel trouble about to happen," he said.

"I guess men don't have that kind of intuition," I replied, wanting to say something clever and right.

"I'd sure as hell like to think we do, Bill. I've been getting some pretty strong vibes lately." He took the CPT flier from the folder. "This has a lot to do with my jitters. I came in at five A.M. a few days ago to get some work done, make a few overseas calls, and coming through the shop I see this guy—a young black guy—taping this to the wall. I wouldn't have thought too much of it if he hadn't looked at me and run." He stopped abruptly, looking at me beseechingly. It was making me uncomfortable. I wanted to tell him what I knew, but I couldn't bring the information from my mind to my mouth. So instead I said something like, "Did you recognize him?"

"No. I was a little too far away and my eyes aren't what they used to be. But I'm sure the kid was black."

"Hmm, I just don't know what to make of this."

"The kid ran when he saw me. Why would he do that if he had nothing to hide? People hang fliers around here all the time."

"Well, what do you think it's all about? You seem more worried about this than I would have thought you'd be."

"Like I told you, I have a feeling. I don't know what it's all about. I was hoping you could tell me that."

"Me? I have no idea. Why should I know?" I was sure he was going to implicate me.

"Well, you're out and about around here more than I am. That's another disadvantage of this job; I don't get out of this damned office enough. I used to know most everyone out in the shop. Not anymore, though. I felt pretty certain that you would have a better rapport—especially with the blacks—than I, or Townes, or Lloyd would." He looked at his watch. "Let me be blunt, Bill; the guy I saw was black. So I have to believe what's going on involves blacks. I'd like you to ask around, see what you can find out. I didn't want to bring this up in staff. There are some potential loose cannons on deck and the last thing I want is a rumor spreading that I'm snooping around on the black workers in this company."

I of course agreed to help in any way I could. I left his office knowing that he had been hedging. He had every reason to be concerned. But how did he know that?

twelve

I'm analyzing hair. Don't ask me why that topic has suddenly emerged as significant. Perhaps it's just the wandering of an addled mind. It's been three days since Paula was last here. I do love her! I do! I can't make her understand. Everything seems to have such an ironic importance now. And lying here, I remember things long forgotten. I have no control over it. My mind seems to trigger to the strangest things.

Today they put screens over the gutters to keep the birds from building nests. So that's the end of Mom and Pop Starling. I think they'd given up anyway. The city can do that to even the most modest ambitions. I'm not feeling very well right now. I think they've done something to my medicine. If Donna were here I'd ask her; she's the only one I can trust. But something is definitely wrong. I'm sweating. It's almost like an anxiety attack, the way they used to be. God, no more voices! I need to calm myself.

I dreamt about my father last night. I almost never think about him. I don't know if it's really him I remember or a photograph of him. You wouldn't believe how strange it is to only remember my father's face as being younger than mine is now. It made me think about hair because one of the only things I remember about my father is a story he told me once about sweeping the hair from the floor of my grandmother's shop. But it was you who asked that question. I remember that about you. I don't have many childhood memories that don't involve you. There was a question you asked about hair once a long time ago. I'm feeling queasy and sweating now. My body is as tense as a knot.

They're supposed to come in with my medicine but they haven't shown up yet. Where is Donna? Did I tell you it was like a bee sting? It was like a bee sting to the head. The sound, the explosive little snap, was just a little louder than a twenty-two, more bass. The sound made it seem bigger, but it felt like a bee sting, like a white-faced hornet from that gray paper nest in Mrs. Francine's pear tree. We can't go there today. She told me to come by the beauty shop first. The brain itself has no sense of touch, it only interprets sensation from other parts of the body. That's why it was like a sting, because it pierced my skull so quickly. But didn't you want to ask her a question?

You can stop by with me. We can walk. We're fifth graders now. Is this something we've already done, stopping by my grandmother's beauty shop, I mean? No, not today? I want some change so we can buy Mary Janes or chewin' wax. The room smells like burnt hair and rotten eggs inside, and why are all these women smoking cigarettes? What are they all laughing about? It's almost like Nisey and them girls all together at recess. They enjoyed a comfort with one another that I was altogether unfamiliar with. Don't ask her that, she might get mad. You're always askin' stuff. You asked her anyway, that question I will never forget. You said, "How come those women come in your beauty shop to have that stinky stuff put in their hair?"

She's looking at you with a mean look. I tol' ju, I tol' ju! See, now we won't get no change! It was as if you had spoken with the tongue of the devil himself. She found the question neither cute nor precocious. She took it almost as an insult. I think she's mad at you now. I don't know why. Why did you have to say it? We won't get no change now!

It wasn't anger, though, it was more embarrassment, wasn't it? She was embarrassed about the fact that you had asked a question that no one in the room could answer without some level of self-consciousness. To answer the question honestly would have been to acknowledge a quiet and long-standing acquiescence to an ideal of attractiveness that they aspired to and were imprisoned by. It put restrictions on how they could think about themselves. It would subordinate them. To sport a natural style would have been unthinkable to those women then (and in large part to their daughters and granddaughters now). In the business world, it's seen as unfeminine and slightly radical—a sign that this person might not be a team player. Nice middle-class black women (and those who aspire to that status) don't wear their hair in short Afros, braids, or dreadlocks; the acceptable thing to do is straighten the hair with chemicals and hot combs so that in texture and style it approximates that of white women.

What was her answer to your question?

"They come in here so they won't walk round lookin' like pickaninnies I guess." She gave me fifty cents and hurried us out the door. She would never admit it, but I don't think she ever forgave you for that question. My grandmother was known to hold a grudge.

This sweating is getting out of control. I'm a little scared. I'm starting to get stomach cramps. At least I can't hear her this time. In the apple orchard you would laugh. We can't shoot anything for your laughing. I mean, you were laughing so much I was afraid the doves wouldn't fly over. You told me they were coming for the seeds of the rotting apples. I remember that smell. We lay in the high grass waiting and I could smell the apples. I'd already found the magazine and when you jumped up to shoot, I looked at you. It wasn't until the creek that you said it. You had to say it, didn't you? Did I ever tell you how you looked, standing there in the middle of the water? Man, do you know you were all I had? Why couldn't you have just kept your mouth shut? I wouldn't have asked.

I'll be back. I haven't forgotten your question. Oh, did I tell you? Remember the project I mentioned in the beginning, the one I had abandoned? Well, I've decided on a method.

thirteen

I opened my eyes this morning thinking I was back in my bed at home. My pillow was damp with sweat, but I was clean. My tongue was sore. There was this salty, slightly metallic taste in my mouth. Donna was there, looking at me strangely. I tried to talk; my speech was worse. I didn't know if it was because my tongue was swollen or something more serious. I formed a question in my mind. And Donna seemed to know. I said it anyway: "Hat aaben?"

She wiped the sweat from my forehead. She told me I was okay, that I had a mild seizure during the night and that the doctors would be talking to me. She smiled; she told me to relax. Then she left. She promised she'd be back.

Later I heard a conversation in the hall. I think they thought I was resting, but I heard the word "relapse" mentioned with a kind of wagging seriousness.

"Why wasn't he under someone's care? Whose decision was it to take him off the medication?"

"Traendofilos is the physician; he's in New York for a few days."

"It was his decision to take him off the medication?"

"He wasn't off completely, the dosage was scaled back.

He seemed like less of a risk. He seemed better, calmer. Something got him agitated."

"The scar tissue on the brain could account for the seizures."

"We're checking that out but we're pretty certain that's what it was. He's had mild ones before but never like this. This is the first one he's had in a few months."

"Where's the wife? She'll want to talk to someone. Where's ah—what's his name?"

"Traendofilos? He's out of town, remember?"

"Oh, that's right. Until next week, right?"

"We're still deciding how we'll proceed with Mrs. Covington."

"What? I don't understand. A wife's going to want to see her husband. I guess we'll have to talk to her first."

"He had asked not to see her."

"Who, Covington?"

"That's right. We don't want him to get agitated again. It's a risk."

"Then maybe she doesn't need to see him, just us. Let's go to my office. He should be sleeping for a while. Tell the nurse, that black one. He seems to be comfortable with her." I was struggling to hear at this point. "Don't forget to tell her we've changed his medication."

fourteen

I've been sleeping a lot. I guess it's the new stuff they're giving me. There isn't much of me you would recognize. The left side of my face is now paralyzed in a permanent grimace (it kind of goes with the hairless gash on the side of my head). There is a slight problem with drool. Despite Donna's efforts, I've lost a lot of weight. Call it my retro-infancy.

My mind is now a colander separating sentiment from remnant obligations. I'm resolving things, or at least identifying things that need resolution. There are priorities for the time left, the time I've allowed myself. Like I told you, I've decided on a method. What is left now is the contemplation of the act—envisioning the moment over and over again in my mind, knowing in reality it will only be experienced and never seen.

Donna says that my disposition has changed. She can be no more specific than that, she tells me. But her suspicions can have consequences, so I must be careful. Yesterday she sang a song to me (she actually has a very nice voice). She called it the "Redemption Song"; I thought it was an old hymn I hadn't heard of, but she said it was island music.

She told me that she lives by that song but that not enough of us in the States have heard it. She said it was time for all of us to reach a new "cognitive phase." She talks this way sometimes. She's spooky. I never quite understand it all. I imagine sometimes that she's the secret leader of some underground movement offering hope and a rigorous, ascetic life. In different circumstances she might have persuaded me to join the cause—but it's too late.

Earlier today I listened to her music again, a tape she said was inspirational. It was also island music, I don't remember the artist. During my physical therapy she slipped the headphones of her Walkman over my ears. I listened as she led my legs and arms through the usual routine of stretches and contortions. Later, back in my room, she told me that the artist I'd listened to was a prophet. One song I remember was called "Buffalo Soldier." I had no idea what it was about, but I liked its mantic energy and rhythm.

I had once believed that Donna was in love with me. I know now that what I'd seen was concern. She's been trying to teach me something all along. Once, after I had described my Jaguar to her in loving detail, she referred to it as my prop. I wish I had her scorn of artifice, her appreciation for the beauty and strength in unadorned things. But I don't. For me to say otherwise would be a pretense. We are acculturated to want and consume beyond need. I don't know what makes Donna different, but I think it's that utilitarian turn of mind that attracted me to her.

Dr. Theodore is back. I know now that he never really left. He talked to me briefly. He wanted to know, among other things, if I was up to seeing Paula today. I thought it was time, so I agreed. She came in just before dinner. I can't get used to the way she looks pregnant. A few times she caught me staring at her stomach, and she quickly averted her eyes. It was as if she didn't want to acknowledge that I was aware of her pregnancy. I guess that's understandable after what I said to her the last time she was here. I wrote a question down for her. I thought communicating through notes would be easier on her than trying to interpret my speech. I wanted to know if she'd felt any movement yet. She smiled a smile I hadn't seen in a long time—happy, but tinged with caution. She didn't stay long, maybe forty-five minutes. Other than my one written question, there was no real attempt at communication. We just sat there like children waiting indoors for the rain to stop. In her good-bye kiss, suspicion lingered like an aftertaste. Perhaps it was more the way she pulled away from me—a tentativeness. Her expression was one of contained shock, as if she were seeing me for the first time.

Sometimes I envision her after they discover me, after she has passed through shock, through anger, through bewilderment to that bottomless state of questioning. The uncertainty and just plain wondering why flowing through her, keeping pace with the sweep of time. I'll become a monument to the tragedy of her life, chiseled in thought.

She'll never see the truth of it. She'll never see how that gravity-defying fiction we created for ourselves collapsed around us. And all that baby has to look forward to is more of the same. The same eventual alienation, the same de facto isolation, the same inescapable sentence of unbelonging, of being thingafied. The same tired grueling dilemma of self-definition. I try not to let myself think about that. There isn't much more time; must rest now.

fifteen

It's taken me a while to collect myself. I tried to keep you apprised as much as was possible. With the new physical-therapy regimen and medication I've been too drained to continue at length. But I'm feeling much better now. And as I said yesterday, there isn't much time.

So where had I left you? Haviland's office? Yes, that's right. Well things really started to shatter for me in the days that followed my meeting with Haviland. I tried frantically to contact Carl. I wanted him to know that the fliers had been noticed. My motivations were self-serving. I wanted to be sure that I wasn't implicated in anything. But Carl had disappeared. What I eventually learned was that he had taken three days' vacation. When I got the answering machine at his home, I began to formulate my own contingencies. Twice I picked up the phone to call Haviland's office only to hang up after the first two digits. At this point, I can say now that I was absolutely unsure about everything— why Carl had disappeared, why I had simply not told Haviland what I knew, why I could no longer make love to my wife.

Then on Monday there was a message waiting on my

desk when I got in. It read simply I'M BACK. WE MUST TALK. MEET ME AT PHILLIPS AT THE HARBOR AT 11:30. He hadn't signed it but I knew it was from him. I could hear him saying the words as I read them. I had no idea what he meant by being "back" or what his urgency was all about. Many wild unnerving possibilities ran through my mind. I can see now how everything sooner or later became another part of the larger paranoia, advancing around me like an ink blot on a crisp white shirt.

Of course the continuing problem of my impotence had its own part in that. It loomed above everything else that was happening, daring to be confronted, taunting me. I had another appointment with Dr. Chang at one o'clock. More tests. Anticipation has a way of dilating the emotional value of any event. My visions of pain were populated with tubes inserted into my penis, bitter liquids, and blood. As a placebo for my fear, I tried to convince myself that lunch with Carl would be relaxing. But I knew better.

Parking at the harbor was always a chore at lunchtime. I had to drive to the roof of the Hyatt's garage to find a space. The leaden sky, which had been threatening all day, was now beginning to deliver a cold light drizzle. I sat for a moment in the car, watching it come down. Almost like a mist it was, falling so fine and airy—more alighting than falling really. And as I left the car, there was something in the feel of the mist against my face (yes, I'm sure of that now) some quality it possessed, a coolness harkening to the feel of creek water just past Indian summer, scents of dead leaves and damp dead fallow fields, of the sharp sickly sweetness of rotting apples in late September—all there, suspended within each particle of that vaporlike drizzle. A door opened before me, battered and yellowing like an old hound's tooth, and as I took the elevator down to the third parking level, I became aware of a question taking form— congealing, clotting like blood from a wound. It had not yet crystallized into even so much as an idea. But I felt it, and it felt like being on the brink of recollection. I walked unimpeded by this awareness, walked from the elevator and then across the footbridge that stretched over Light Street into the first harbor pavilion.

I made my way through the crowd, passing the raw bar where a group of old black men drank beer and swallowed fresh-shucked oysters from the half shell. There was already a line leading into Phillips and as I came up to the hostess's station, I saw Carl right away, sitting alone at a table in the center of the restaurant, staring out over the harbor as he took a last drag on a cigarette.

He didn't bother to look up at me as I approached, but seemed instead to sense my presence. Even when I came up to the table and pulled out a chair, he maintained his dreamy gaze across the water. "I can't believe what they've done with this waterfront," he said. "Ten years ago this place was a dump." Then he turned to look at me. "Nice tie. Valentino, isn't it?"

"Tino Cosma; Paula picked it up. Look, I hope you're not expecting me to talk about ties today."

"No, and I didn't mean to leave you such an ambiguous message, but I was in a rush this morning. I have some interesting news to share."

"Well, I've got news too; I've had it for a while now. Where the hell have you been, Carl? I've been trying to reach you since last week."

"I know. I've gotten messages from you all over town. I had to go out West. Haim got hurt on his skateboard. Some drunk Mexican asshole riding around in the evening without headlights ran into him."

"Good Lord! I'm sorry. Is he okay? Is he hurt badly?"

"Broken leg, a few bruises. It could have been a lot worse. Marcia had no business taking those kids so far away from me. And you'd think with the money I send her every month she'd live in a less congested part of town."

Our waitress came by and we ordered drinks (a bourbon and water for me, a rum and Coke for Carl). He talked in more detail about his son's accident and then about his daughter's ballet classes. His voice had a pained elongated tone, as if every word spoken had arrived after traveling some great distance. When the drinks came I ordered fried soft-shell crabs and Carl got the swordfish steak. There was a brief silence. He was still thinking about his children, I realized, and it was consuming him. At that moment he must have noticed that he was sinking into some bottomless torpor because he abruptly brought the conversation back to business.

"So why all the messages, Billy?" As he said that I noticed a stack of papers on the chair between us. I could only see that they were photocopied sheets. My first thought was that he'd brought the fliers with him, and my whole body went warm, sweaty and light with a rush of adrenaline.

"Do you really think it's smart to walk around here with those? Anyone could see you." I pointed to the chair.

"What, these?" he said, looking down to the stack and then thrusting a handful of papers into my face. I could see now that what I thought were fliers were only copies of an expense-report form. "I'm not going to call you paranoid, Billy, because you already know you are."

"I've got cause. You weren't here last week. Haviland brought one of your fliers to his staff meeting."

"So what?" he said, sipping his drink. "So he saw a flier.

We knew they would be seen. He doesn't know what they mean—unless you told him. You didn't, did you?"

"No, I haven't said anything—yet. But you don't understand. He saw the kid hanging them up."

"The kid? You mean Everett? Who saw him, Haviland?"

"Yeah, Haviland. He saw him hanging one up in manufacturing. And worse yet, Everett took off when he saw Haviland. Now he's very interested in the fliers."

"He ran from Haviland? Oh shit! Damn! Did Haviland recognize him? Of course not. So what did he say when he brought it up?"

"Like I said, the whole thing's got him bugged now. He even asked me privately, after staff, if I knew anything about the fliers."

"And you didn't say anything?"

"I told you I didn't!"

"All right, all right, I just needed to know for sure."

"You've set me out on a pretty flimsy limb, Carl. I don't like the way this thing feels at all. I think Haviland knows more than he's letting on."

"You are paranoid, Billy. How could he know anything—unless you told him?"

"Damn it, I didn't say anything! I'm reconsidering though! You know that? I'm reconsidering the whole goddamned niggerish mess right this minute!" I had spoken a bit too loudly and more than a few faces turned our way.

"Okay, okay," he said in a lowered tone. "The question is what are we going to do now?"

"We? We aren't going to do anything. This one's all yours. I don't know about you, Carl, but I have a career at stake." That sobered him up. His smugness seemed to collapse under the weight of my statement. "Haviland is groping around for information now. It won't be long before he puts something together. Lloyd's already been looking into the fliers for him. Yeah, and that's another thing. Lloyd just kind of disappeared after the meeting. I haven't seen him in three days."

"Lloyd? You need to calm down, Billy; I mean it. You really think Lloyd dug up information for Haviland? Who the hell would tell Lloyd anything? And after what I found out about—"

"I haven't seen him for three days! Didn't you hear what I said, three days! And who knows what he's doing."

"Well, you can sleep soundly tonight because he was in my office this morning. He wanted to tell me about a new business proposition he has. He wants to develop a pill that will make a fart smell like a rose. Now does that sound like the conversation of a superspy? Get a grip, Billy. I've never seen you like this before. Lloyd Harrow is chicken shit! He wanders up and down the halls looking for someone whose time he can waste. In fact that's what I wan—"

"Well, what are you going to do about Everett? It's only a matter of time before Haviland spots him again. He'll ask me something again! What are you going to do about that, huh?"

"What are you going to do about it, Billy? What are you going to say? I hope you don't say anything to Haviland. I hope I can count on that. I'm going to have to speed things up. There's a meeting Thursday. We'll have to decide what's next then. You should be there too, Billy—impress upon everyone how urgent this thing is." He drank the last of his rum and Coke.

"Are you crazy? Have you absolutely lost your mind? I'm already more involved in this than I want to be. I'm not coming to any meeting. And you're the one setting up these meetings, aren't you?"

"You're already involved! Haviland involved you—and you work for him, remember?"

"You involved me! And you didn't answer my question."

"What difference does it make, Billy? The question now is what are you going to do? That's the only real question here." And I became aware again of the other question, still there, still composing itself. It was like waiting to remember.

At that moment the waitress arrived with our food. Carl ordered a cup of coffee and I asked for another bourbon. I thought he was waiting for me to answer him, which I couldn't do since I had no answer. But he surprised me.

"Look, Billy," he sighed, "let's drop this for now, okay? I didn't ask you here to put you on the spot." This was a bizarre turn of events. Thinking back on it now, I guess he was just hedging his bets. He may have been afraid of treading too heavily on whatever fragile bond we shared. Perhaps he had the notion that I might come around to joining him, and that pressing me would only ensure it would never happen. Whatever his motivations at the time, he turned the conversation from Varitech to food.

He became very interested in my lunch. The soft-shell crabs were small—I knew they would be—but they had given me three of them. And while, as I explained to Carl, they couldn't rival what I remembered my grandmother frying up in bacon grease some Saturday afternoon long ago, they didn't really look too bad. All three were a light uniform brown, and even the rye was toasted dark, the way I like it. Carl watched as I assembled the sandwich, first laying down a sparse bed of lettuce on the rye and then topping that with two thick slices of tomato, a touch of salt and pepper, and then the crabs themselves. He laughed a little at the meticulous way I placed the crabs side by side on the bread, like tongue-and-groove planking. On the crowning slice of rye, I spread a hearty swath of Dijon and then pressed everything together as best I could.

"I could never work up the stomach to eat one of those," he said, cutting into his swordfish steak.

"Well then you don't know what you're missing. Or don't you like the taste of crabs?"

"I like crabs fine. But those ... I've only seen people eating those up here. What, do they just cook the whole thing, legs and all?"

"More or less. You just lift up the top shell, cut out the lungs, cut off the face, and then fry the rest of the crab. A soft-shell crab is just a regular ole blue crab that's shed its shell. I used to net them in the eel grass when I was a boy."

"I guess it's the legs hanging out from between the bread and all. It makes it look ... I don't know, unsettling. Yeah, to a country boy raised on grits and biscuits it's unsettling to eat a sandwich with legs hanging out from under it."

We went on with this flummery until we were near the end of the meal. I looked at my watch. I still had Dr. Chang to contemplate. There were only about twenty-five minutes left to walk back to the car and drive to his office.

"Do you realize we haven't talked yet about why I asked you here?" Carl said. "Aren't you curious?"

"I guess I'm more afraid than curious. Is this going to be another bombshell, like the fliers and the strike you've mixed me up in?"

I remember how his bottom lip quivered at that, but instead of saying anything that might set us arguing in an unwanted direction, he lit up another cigarette.

"It's about Lloyd," he said. "I've been trying to tell you all along but you were too busy into your premenstrual bitch thing to let me finish."

"So can you walk and talk?" I said. We both got up to

leave. Carl insisted on paying the tab and after mild objection I let him. He was also parked in the garage at the Hyatt, so as we walked along together he began to speak his piece about Lloyd. I was trying to balance my attention between listening and that same sensation of being on the brink of recollection. It was like waiting to remember.

He began with what I'd call rhetorical information—the circumstance of Lloyd's banishment to Baltimore, the position he'd held in Philly.

"And I guess you know about his family," he said. "They own one of the largest banks in eastern Pennsylvania. His father owns a lot of our stock. His aunt is on our board of directors. I wouldn't be surprised if the Harrows owned the damned Liberty Bell. They're old money, old old money."

We were on the footbridge now, crossing back over Light Street. I realized that the scent of apples I smelled was coming from the old McCormick plant next door. The light drizzle had graduated to a steady rain. We stopped just inside the entrance of the garage and I heard the sound of water—running, dripping, echoing through the place, giving it a haunting cavernous quality. It seemed to me, at that moment, to be the most desolate place on earth.

"Drugs is what I heard," he said finally. "And you didn't hear it from me."

"Man, they've kept that quiet, haven't they!" I said. "I knew it had to be something like that."

"Yeah, well apparently your superspy had a big-time cocaine habit. It got so bad he was missing work, blowing up in meetings, accusing people of sabotaging his projects—you know how that stuff warps you."

"I've heard."

"It got pretty bad with him. He got busted at a party trying to make a buy. Now here's a guy with access to military programs so sensitive he has secret clearance, and he's picked up at a party trying to buy drugs. You know if he were black it would have been all over the news."

Two men dressed in trench coats and carrying briefcases approached us from the walkway. Carl went silent until they passed.

"They sent him off to the Betty Ford Center—or some-place like that—to dry out."

"So how did he end up on Haviland's staff? I'd like to know how they work those kinds of deals."

"We'll probably never know that. We don't get those kind of concessions. 'Cause this is definite crazy white people's stuff. Why would a guy like Lloyd be doing coke? Think about it. You can almost understand some down-and-out brother selling the stuff for money, or using it like alcohol, but what kind of pressure is Lloyd under?"

"Something to do?" I said. "I don't know. Maybe he can't touch the money, who knows? Maybe Varitech gets to him like it gets to you?" We stood waiting for the elevator. "So how did you find this all out, Carl?"

"You don't believe me?" he said, lighting another cigarette.

"I didn't say that! I believe you all right. I'm just curious. How did you find out?"

"Selma King. Her brother-in-law works in the Philly office. He heard it firsthand from a guy who worked for Lloyd. Now, I'm telling you all of this so you can watch out. I know you've gone to car shows and places like that with him, but you don't want to get too associated with Mr. Superspy."

"I appreciate your concern about my career but—"

"Hey, I just don't want to see you 'locked into a dead-end job with no chance of promotion.'" He smiled his sheepish smile. "Think again about coming to the meeting."

I shrugged. Then the elevator arrived. This car would be mine; it was going up.

"So...maybe I'll see you at the meeting?" Carl said as I stepped onto the elevator, already so intent on waiting to remember that I barely heard him.

"Don't count on it!" I shouted as the doors closed, not really knowing if he had heard me.

. . .

Pregna Chainsukh smiled this time as I walked up to the reception desk. We were alone in the waiting area today.

"You are very pountual Mistier Covintin." She smiled. "It ees exactly won o'clouk."

"So, do you always remember everyone's name?" I said. I hadn't meant to jump on her. But for a second her comment had sounded like a condemnation.

She heard the acrimony in my voice, and at the instant she looked up, I think she saw something in my face too, something of my bewilderment and indignation. I suppose to the sane insanity is more baffling than anything else.

"Eits thaat you our so tol," she said, sheepishly almost, as if to redress what she had seen in my face. "Doctier Chong will be aout in a mooment."

But now I couldn't let it go at that. I tried to correct myself with conversation rather than let my embarrassment wax in silence. Fourteen years at Varitech had given me that skill too.

"Those are interesting earrings," I said. I have no idea where this stuff comes from. I just open my mouth and it's there. The earrings were really nothing special—two copper disks suspended on thick chains.

"You like them? They are a geift from my fathier, from Ceylon." I pretended to study the earrings, nodding approv-

143

ingly, creating a brief silence before I asked my next question.

"Is that where you're from, Ceylon?"

"I am from everywhere." She laughed. "No, Ceylon is jist wheir my fathier is now. I was born oun Cyprus."

"Oh, then you're Greek—or Turkish?"

She laughed again. "That would be an exploseive combinaation. I dount know what I am. My fathier is from Surat and my mothier is from Khartoum. What does that make me?" At that moment I had a recognition. I saw a glimpse of what I was still waiting to remember. It was in her remark, or her remark was part of it. It was only a flash and I couldn't know for sure.

I might have stood there all day in feverish rumination, but Dr. Chang took that moment to make his appearance, dour and deliberate, perfunctory in his greeting. He handed Pregna a stack of papers and then escorted me back into his office. I took a chance at conversation hoping to offset the strangeness of my behavior.

"Your receptionist is a very interesting woman."

"Pregna? In what way?" Oddly enough he seemed genuinely interested.

"Her appearance, the way she talks. She's just a bit beyond your common smiling blonde," I said. He laughed. He actually laughed.

"We've been married so long; I guess I've just gotten used to that." I'm sure my jaw dropped. Arleigh didn't say anything about a wife. Of course this new fact eventually fueled my paranoia. I envisioned my case discussed over the dinner table. I convinced myself that she knew. Talking to her again would be awkward. How I would handle that became another point of tension.

When we got into his office, Dr. Chang had me undress and take a seat on the examination table. "Let's see," he said, clipboard in hand, "how have things been going? Any changes? Have you noticed anything different?"

I thought in earnest for a second. "No, nothing's changed."

"Well, today we'll begin the IVP workup. That's the test to check blood flow through your kidneys and testicles, in case you forgot. And I'd like you to think about checking into University Hospital soon for the NPT test."

"I'm sorry, I don't remember what that one is either."

"Nocturnal penile tumescence. Remember? That's the test to see if you are having erections in your sleep. It's pretty simple. We hook up monitors to your body and you go to sleep and we see what happens."

"Is this a one-time thing? I mean how many times will I have to do this?"

"Not more than two or three times. The sooner we get started, the better." He looked at his clipboard. "Any chance you could make it on Thursday night?"

"I don't see why not. What time should I be there?"

He gave the details and then wrote something down on the clipboard. He told me whom to ask for, where I should go. He also told me not to take any medication or drink any alcohol for at least eight hours before the test.

"It's very ironic," he added, "but the things our culture promotes as a part of the sex act—you know, the drink before, the cigarette after—are two of the worst things you can do for your sex life. Nicotine and alcohol wreak havoc on pelvic nerves and blood vessels."

I wondered if he said that because he smelled alcohol on my breath.

My examination that day was only mildly uncomfortable; not at all what I had anticipated. As I prepared to leave, I was told to expect a little more discomfort next time. Dr. Chang escorted me back to the reception area. I already knew I wouldn't be able to look Pregna in the eye, and there was a certain anxiety in that knowledge. But Pregna was nowhere to be found. Dr. Chang scheduled my next visit, at which time I would get the results of the NPT test.

The sales conference and Dr. Chang's own commitments forced us to schedule my next appointment much later in the month. I didn't know then that I wouldn't make it. We shook hands and I left.

The rain was now coming down in sheets and I was without an umbrella. My grandmother used to call it hot soup weather. I thought of that as I pulled the collar of my London Fog up around my neck. I thought how ironic it was that, given the choice, I'd have preferred bourbon over soup that day. I had parked in the Center Street lot again. It would be a wet four-block walk. I started out briskly at first, feeling the rain, and then remembering the question, waiting for it. But it was still coming, still beyond the scope of language or remembering.

Then something happened that stopped me dead and knotted me with a panic that I wouldn't have thought possible. Just past the Washington Monument, I heard a voice. I thought it said, *Ain't nothin' but niggerishness.*

I was unable to move. For not only did the voice seem to emanate from all points at once, it almost sounded like my grandmother's voice. I looked around frantically and then I heard it a second time and I was sure: *Ain't nothin' but niggerishness.* My heart was beating as if ready to burst through my chest. I was having trouble catching my breath. It's hard to describe the abject sense of isolation I felt at that moment. Something like the feeling I had standing in the parking garage earlier with Carl, the same general sense of detachment, but more intense now. It was as if I'd been snatched from my rainy Baltimore street and without warning placed at the bottom of the ocean. I began to gasp for breath, wanting to call out for help but unable to find the air in my chest. I was terrified. I couldn't swallow. I even came close to urinating on myself. Then my head began to spin. I was able to plop down on one of the benches near the monument. Slowly, I began to compose myself. Breathing became easier until I was alone in the rain; just alone in the rain, I told myself.

Coming up the hill toward me was a woman and two small children. At first I wasn't sure it was real until I saw it was the same trio I'd passed on my last visit to Dr. Chang. She was under a pink umbrella, the boys wearing drenched Oriole caps and thin blue windbreakers that looked like black plastic garbage bags, they were so slick with rain. As they got closer, what I had taken to be a scarf on the woman I could now see was a wig. I don't think it could have been her own hair. I don't think it's possible to dye black hair that color. It was as white as a piano key, fashioned in that wispy pulled-over style that Marilyn Monroe made famous in *The Seven Year Itch*. I must have been quite a sight to them as well, because they all stared at me as they passed.

That's when I saw her eyes. They were blue. It didn't even dawn on me right away that she was looking at me through blue contacts. Even now, sometimes when I close my eyes, I can still see her, and hear her, for just as she passed me she screamed.

"Jamal! You betta git yo black ass outta that gotdamned worta! Is you lost ya mine!"

He had been walking in the torrents rushing down along the gutter between the sidewalk and the street. I knew what he wanted. He wanted to know what it felt like, how cold it was, what sound it made as it passed and splashed over the laces of his shoes, soaking him to his socks. I felt for him because I understood why he would walk in the water. I saw myself as a boy, you and I both, standing under the leaky rainspouts of your mother's house during late summer rains, free and happy for as long as we could feel the water moving. And then there you were, Paul Walker, seventeen years old, standing in the middle of the creek about to ask the question incubating in my brain, becoming fluid—part of the rain against my face. Then you were finally just standing there, watching me back away...back...back. I heard a car horn. A few people driving by slowed down to stare. I got up, a little wobbly, and started toward my car again, shaking from fear and cold. Once inside, I turned the heat up as far as it would go. There was no way I could go back to work. I pulled off the lot and began to make my way up Charles Street.

I had barely begun to regain myself when again I heard *Ain't nothin' but niggerishness*. I was waiting at the light at Charles and University and I gripped the sides of the seat with all my might. I squeezed until I started to sweat, until my fingers burned. I was unable to move. There was this knowledge from somewhere that if I released the seat something terrible would happen. The light changed and I sat there. Horns blew, cars went around me, irate drivers with their middle fingers pressed hard against their windows. I could hear the rain falling in heavy drops, splattering on the roof of the car with an almost rhythmically calculated violence. The light changed a second time, and I was able to pull off.

When I got to Alonzo's I called out for my bourbon and water before I'd taken a seat at the bar. People stared. Larry the bartender, who knew me as a regular, put my drink down in front of me and asked if everything was okay. I told him—loud enough for all to hear—that I had skidded in the rain and just avoided totaling my car. I don't know how or when I'd become so adept at lying. But everyone bought my story, and as conversation broke out around the bar about accidents experienced and observed, I was left to drink in peace. And drink I did. If any talk was directed my way, I didn't hear it. I started to feel at ease after my second drink, coaching myself to relax. Alonzo's was a good place to relax. Its amenities included a good-natured staff, monstrous hamburgers, and a genial loquacious crowd. Although it could occasionally get noisy and double as a kind of nice people's pickup bar, it was not rowdy and never brazen. It's what a neighborhood bar should be—a warm homey place to get drunk. It was also just a few blocks from my house, so I could walk home if need be. And that's what I ended up doing that afternoon. I pretty much drank until I was almost out of money. Then I just sat there until I was sure Paula was home. I didn't want to be in the house alone. I guess I was afraid.

I left my car on Keswick Street. For the second time that day I walked four blocks in the rain and got soaked. In true drunkard fashion I fumbled to get my key in the lock, finally resigning myself to ringing the bell. Paula must have been expecting me because she yanked the door open without asking who was there. Inside, she didn't say a word to me. Even after I said hello and attempted a kiss. She told me there was chicken in the refrigerator and then added, "Or did you have something to eat at Alonzo's?"

That was all she said to me that evening, besides mumbling something about my acting like an asshole after a visit to the doctor. I later figured that she must have seen my car parked near the bar. I showered and went to bed without eating. Paula was already asleep, curled up under the covers like an unhatched chick. She flinched when I tried to coax her body next to mine. I wanted to wrap myself around her, partly as an offer of reconciliation but also because she was soft and warm, a safe harbor. But she wouldn't allow it, even after I reminded her of some advice her mother once gave us.

"Remember," I said, "she told us we should never go to bed angry."

"It would be nice to think that's possible," she mumbled.

It's easy to look back now and ask all the right questions. Why didn't I tell Paula what happened? Why didn't I seek help for the attack I'd had? Why did I write it all off the next morning as the result of fatigue, a freak occurrence? The only thing harder than asking those questions then would be answering them now. I couldn't give you a why for most of the things I did. I can only tell you what happened. Any meaning you apply will be your own.

Over the next few days, things at work began collapsing by degrees. Gordy told me that Howie Frost had shot down the wave-solder ad—not totally unexpected. And on Thursday, Nancy brought the news that Dierdre had come down with chicken pox and would be out for at least two weeks.

"I guess she never had them as a child," Nancy said.

We'd now be a body short at the sales conference. There was also another CPT flier on my desk. I knew the code now. This one probably referred to the meeting Carl was now forced to call. He'd written BE THERE in red across the bottom of the sheet. I also had a stack of phone messages from the day before. One from Carl, one from Lloyd, and most notably, one from John Haviland. Nancy had written WANTS TO SEE YOU ASAP! in the margin.

I got up immediately. The only thing Haviland could want to know was what I'd found out about the fliers. Again, I began to envision various scenarios. Some had me telling Haviland everything I knew; others had me withholding the same information entirely.

Then it came creeping back. That sense of desolation first, and then her voice. This time she said, *You know what you gotta do*. I braced myself against the wall, losing my breath, looking around to see that there was no one else in the hall. This time I forced myself to walk. The shortness of breath eased quickly. She kept repeating herself. I looked up; I looked around. It was growing louder. I kept walking. She wouldn't stop. It was becoming unbearable. I kept telling myself it wasn't there, but that didn't help. I covered my ears; I wanted to poke something in my ears to make it stop. I kept walking. I dug my little finger into my right ear in a frenzied attack. But I could still hear her. I felt something warm against my finger and realized that I'd cut my ear. There was blood on my fingernail. Then suddenly she stopped. I was standing in the doorway of Haviland's office.

Claire looked up and smiled as I came through. Her face quickly twisted into an expression that encompassed both wonder and grave concern.

"What's the matter with you?" she said. I fumbled for a response.

"What do you mean?" I replied, trying to sound as if I had no idea what she was talking about.

"Well, it's like you're in pain or something." I told her I had a splitting headache. She offered me two aspirin. I thanked her and swallowed both without water. "Oh my god!" she said as I turned. "Your ear is bleeding." What explanation could I give for that?

I touched the ear. "My god, you're right. I don't know how that could have happened." I took a tissue from her and after a little more chatting, I asked to see John.

"Oh, didn't you know? He's in New York this week." She was still looking at me cautiously. "He told me to tell you that if he didn't get in touch with you yesterday he'd see you at the sales conference on Sunday evening."

I thanked her for the aspirin again and left. My experience had unsettled me. As usual I hid out in my office for the rest of the day. I didn't go out for lunch; I didn't take any calls. I asked Nancy to tell anyone who came to see me that I couldn't be disturbed.

"Tell anyone who asks that I'm on a conference call with John Haviland," I said. I conducted everything from my office. I even talked to Gordy by phone. Never did I stop to consider how crazy this all must have seemed. Carl called several times, as did Lloyd—long lost Lloyd. I even heard him stop by once to ask Nancy what was going on, to which she dutifully responded with the party line. I don't know what unnamed fear lurked outside my office, but it was enough to keep me from opening the door.

But then I had a something of a surprise guest, one who would not be barred. It was Len Townes. He walked in over Nancy's objections, and when he saw I wasn't really on the phone he smiled with a cynic's delight. It was a smile he seldom allowed these born-again days and I'd almost forgotten the look. He spoke in his calm measured way.

"I see you're done with your call." He turned to Nancy, who was standing in the doorway, first giving me a face that was the nonverbal equivalent of I'm sorry. "Thank you," he said to her politely and then he closed the door.

"I think we have something to talk about, Bill. This thing," he had one of the fliers in his hand. "I think you might know something about these." The way he said it, it didn't really sound like an accusation, but he looked into me for an answer.

"I don't know what you mean."

"Well, I know John asked you about them and I thought you might have found something out."

"No. I haven't. And, well to tell you the truth, Len, I guess I would feel a little uncomfortable saying anything to you before I had a chance to talk to John."

"Now hold on there, mister. He asked me to find out what I could too. I'm just looking at this as a team effort. I know you're a team player, that's all."

"Well, I'm sorry, Len, I just don't know anything. Like I think I told John, whatever that flier is, it has something to do with operations. I would think, well I mean, that you would know more about what was going on there than me."

"Well like I said I'm doing my best to find out. If there's a problem I need to know about it to fix it." He smiled. "But hey, we're on the same team, right? I'll let you get back to whatever you were doing." He started toward the door. "I'm sure I'll see you in Atlanta." Then, almost as an aside, he said, "Guess I'll stop down to talk to Carl Rice for a minute." He looked into me again, this time from the corner of his eyes. "Have you seen him lately; I mean, do you know if he's in today?"

"I couldn't tell you," I said, and he nodded and left.

Soon after that I slipped out for the day. I was too nervous to even wade through the rest of the afternoon. Before I did, I asked Nancy how she felt about taking Dierdre's place in Atlanta. It was short notice, but we could use the help. She seemed pretty excited about the prospect of travel. I told her to have the travel department reissue Dierdre's tickets in her name. That way they would arrive tomorrow along with mine. I signed the necessary paperwork and then left.

I didn't stop by Alonzo's that afternoon. Instead I went straight home—in part because I was scheduled for testing in the sleep lab that night, but also because I was scared. Everything seemed to be collapsing, out of control. I could no longer deny that. Driving home that day I tried for a while to approach the problem analytically, to identify a pattern to the episodes I had experienced, to what was happening at work—my feckless way of imposing a sense of order on the situation. But my reasoning led me to places I feared to tread.

When I got home I curled up on the couch. I began to wonder if my impotence and the anxiety attacks weren't symptoms of something larger—a possibility Dr. Chang had suggested. It seemed logical. But you and I both know that cause and effect aren't easily assigned. And then there was that question, getting closer I felt, quickening now just beyond knowing.

I was still on the couch when Paula walked in. My presence there was enough to startle her into dropping a small bag of groceries. She of course wanted to know why I was home so early. I told her nothing about the episodes. I made up something vague about wanting to prepare for my night at the sleep lab. But she didn't know anything about that. I'd come home drunk the night before and it was never discussed. So in the kitchen, as I helped her put away the things she'd purchased, I talked in detail about my visit with Dr. Chang—including the stay at the sleep lab. She was understandably angry that I hadn't brought it up before, telling me she would have stayed with Karen had she known I'd be away that night. I think my negligence worried her into questioning my long-term itinerary.

"When are you supposed to be going to Atlanta?" she asked.

"Sunday morning. I'll drive the Jag to the airport, park it in valet."

"Are you going to be up to traveling? You're going to be in this lab all of tonight."

"I'll be asleep. All I do there is sleep. Besides, I'll have Saturday to pack and all," I said as I foraged in the refrigerator.

Paula was standing before the sink now, looking out of the kitchen window into Bruce and Steffie's yard, where Bruce and little James were raking leaves. An easy silence surrounded us, not hostile or pensive in any way, just peaceful, almost like an allusion to motionlessness. It was a moment of calm long absent in our home. I came up from behind her and let my arms gently encircle her waist. There was so much to be said. But we just stood there, both of us groping cautiously in our reticence for the words that would give expression to whatever it was we were experiencing.

I watched her remove her earrings—two gold BBs that shimmered like teardrops in the dissolving afternoon light. They were like the silence we shared, a precious golden moment afforded by the brief reflection of some waning star. She removed them in a delicate precise motion, cupping them in her hand like water. Even when she spoke, she tried not to betray the silence, and she didn't because what she really meant, what she actually wanted to say, went unspoken. But I saw it in her face as she watched James jumping up and down in the leaves he and his father had just raked into a pile. I had seen her wear that face while we were shopping down at the harbor once. We were browsing in a pet store where a small boy and his mother had just purchased a kitten. The little boy cried when she told him that he couldn't play with the kitten until they were home. When she picked him up and said, "Now Daniel, hush," Paula wiped a tear from her eye. I played the dutiful fool and pretended not to notice what had happened. But you see, Daniel was the name we had once settled on long ago for our own child. Women just bury their pain in shallower graves, that's all.

When she did finally turn from the window she said, "I guess you'll want something to eat before you leave?"

A little later, while preparing a sandwich for me, she wondered aloud why I didn't hold her anymore.

"Just because we can't have sex doesn't mean we still can't be intimate," she said.

I really don't think she had any idea how deep and close to the bone that statement cut. What was intimacy to lovers without sex, I wanted to ask her! I wasn't interested in another mother figure in my life. I didn't know of any other options for intimacy with a wife. (That was the sad extent of my thinking then.)

I went upstairs, packed a few things, and left with a tight-lipped good-bye. I've come to believe that for a lot of men, rage and reticence can be a way of keeping their fears in remission. You only realize how ineffective and frightened you've been once you're alone with yourself and all your little hairy hobgoblins come out and stare you in the face.

Not so surprising then that I would try to call Paula when I got to the hospital. I got the answering machine. She was either not picking up or she had gone to Karen's house for the night. I would have tried there if I had known the number.

The sleep lab was on the fifth floor of the hospital. The receptionist at the admissions counter was a large, late-fiftyish-looking woman, whose even larger red hair was truly the color of the flame from a disposable lighter. She told me I had to fill out a series of forms before I could go up. I kept noticing the smell. She smelled like cumin seed, a pungent musky smell just a little like fresh sweat. I wondered if it was a new perfume or some more significant comment on femininity. Or maybe she just suffered from poor hygiene. It worried me vaguely. I'd always associated medical places and mortuaries with a certain antiseptic smell of scrubbed and formaldehyded lifelessness. I had never realized how comforting that smell could be.

When I had finally finished with the forms I took the elevator upstairs. I was surprised at how much the room appeared as I had imagined it would. A little ten by fifteen room with one window facing east toward downtown, gray linoleum floors, a single bed, a small television set, and a one-way observation window. There was an eeriness about it.

An intern (I was sure he was too young to be a doctor) came into the room as I was looking around. He introduced himself as Dr. Bergman. He was a tall articulate white kid, very seasoned in his manner for someone so young. I put my things on the bed and sat down. Then Dr. Bergman began to explain everything to me: the workings of all the electronic machinery (which I couldn't see through the one-way glass), how the sensors would be attached to my body, how the data would be monitored and analyzed. He told me to relax.

By ten I was in bed properly wired up and unable to fall asleep. I was like a child on Christmas Eve, too charged with anticipation to rest. I played an old game, opening and closing my eyes trying to decide if there was any difference between the darkness of the room and the back of my own eyelids.

Sometime during that game I must have fallen asleep because when I opened my eyes again, I was looking out over Roland Avenue. Me, Paula, and the Warings; we were all taking a ride around the neighborhood in the new Benz. Then darkness again and then I was a boy playing in back of my grandmother's shop with you, Walter Perry, Austin Kimball, and Niles Merritt. Walter's dog Fuzzy was even there, barking at the radio the way he used to. You had it up loud because Little Richard was wailing through "Lucille" and you loved that song. You were showing me a new dance step until my grandmother came out and told us to turn down the radio. She called me to the door.

"Don't git too cuftable wit niggerishness, you hear me," she whispered. Her face was not the one of my youth, and I remember my fear very well, for she had the death face I'd seen at her wake. "Nobody neva made nofin' of theyselves strutting round like they afflicted. And I bet you don't see them white kids in school doin' it, do you?"

Then everything began to come in accelerating flashes, as if moving downhill. Carl in front of me, standing in the dry loose dirt, dressed for work, candy bar in hand, the dust settling on his shoes. Carl in back of the beauty shop. The sun high and hot, a humid, draining, emulsifying summer day in Roberts, Maryland. A child, when I spoke to Carl, an adult when he spoke to me. My grandmother, silent, scowling, glaring out from behind a screen door. I could tell she was thinking *Just niggerishness!*

"You think these white people see you as one of them?" Carl said. And then he had Haviland's face but Carl's voice. "Do you really believe that!" *Just plain niggerishness!*

"You've got your job because someone gave their permission for you to take it, that's all. We don't do a thing in America without their permission." *Just plain niggerish!*

"You're what they want to see, a docile, thankful Negro." *Just plain niggerishness!* He was Len Townes now with a crown of plastic thorns and a white polyester suit. "Here's a joke for you, Billy: What do you call a black doctor from Macon? A nigger; get it? You still call him a nigger!"

He walked behind me and he was Carl again, still eating the candy bar. My grandmother's casket was lying out in the sun. Carl walked up to the casket and set a can of Coke on the lid.

"Well," he said, "are you going to bury her or am I?"

When I looked up at the screen door, though, she was still there looking at me sternly, the way she used to look when I had done something she didn't approve of. I looked back at the casket and Carl was Len in the white suit, standing over it. I heard him say the Lord's Prayer and then he kissed her lightly on the forehead. Then I was myself, a man, facing Carl where I'd stood as a boy. But my grandmother was still staring at me from behind the screen, trembling with anger. *Niggerish, niggerish!*

"Don't you see," Carl said quietly. He was himself again now, standing beside a freshly dug grave. "That's why we're black-businessmen, black-policemen, black-actors, black-writers, black-Republicans, black-Americans. We have a hyphenated credibility, a hyphenated humanity, a hyphenated existence. 'Black' can almost stand for 'kind of.'" He looked over to her coffin and then into the grave and then at me. "I'll help you, come on." *Just plain niggerish!*

"But she's not dead," I said.

He was Len speaking now. "You know how to keep a

cracker occupied? Ask him if he'd rather his daughter marry a black or tell him that she's gay. It's like computing pi to the last digit, there's no solution!"

I was on a roadside dressed for work, walking from school with you, yelling, crying until my lungs were cramped and empty: "White kids don't spit on me from school buses anymore! They don't, not like before!" And you looking on and Carl laughing above it all. Len whispering, "We thought for sure it was a nigger," then spitting on me as he passed in my Jaguar.

"It's as real as rain. I can touch everything I have." And Carl laughing: "And you think that's something to brag about!" Dr. Bond looked me in the face, cowering in his library, and said yes.

"I like living a comfortable life," I told my grandmother. She kissed me, saying, "Momma was black as tar but I loved her anyway."

"The master can always call the slave lazy," Carl said. "You ain't doing nothing new, Billy. You're just another brother working for a white man." *Don't git too cuftable wit niggerishness!*

I could smell burning hair and pomade from straightening combs moving through the screen door, I could feel them, their heat swirling around my grandmother's body and then out past my face.

You and I were watching "Star Trek," and Lieutenant Uhura looked at us and said, "How come those advanced alien races that Kirk and Spock run into are always a bunch of white people dressed like Romans? You ever notice that?" And then Spock said, "It's all a paradigm, a paradigm of the white psyche. Everything is. Ultimately it's them in control of themselves. The only aliens of color on 'Star Trek' are the Klingons, the dark, barbaric, violent Klingons."

Carl and I studied his son Haim watching a cartoon called "He-Man." "See," Haim said, "there's He-Man, the most powerful man in the universe." Then he said in his father's voice, "You know how inconceivable it would be to make that character black? Do you know? It would never happen. How can you ignore that evidence? It's all around you, everywhere."

Finally my grandmother stepped out from behind the screen door with Paula, holding a newborn baby. It was sexless, stillborn, scarred and used, flecked with blood. I backed away, a child myself, screaming. She held it up for me to touch and I could smell it festering like spoiled meat. Haviland, Dr. Bond, Len, Carl, and you Paul were all standing there watching, waiting. It was as if she'd opened an oven because heat was singeing my hair, I could smell it burning. And then the very air seemed to dissolve into light, so bright that I had to cover my eyes. I fell to the ground, remembering at that moment, the question coming, almost, almost now, almost ...

The midmorning sun was blazing through my window. I was in the sleep lab, in the little single bed, damp with sweat. I looked at my watch; it was nine A.M. Friday.

Not long after that the sensors were removed from my body and I got dressed and went into the office. I was only planning to stay for a half day. There were still loose ends to tie up before the trip to Atlanta. The plant seemed abandoned. After the confusion of the last few days, this false calm would reinforce the delusion I was trying to build that things weren't as serious as I made them out to be. I guess I was trying to convince myself. It's what I wanted to believe, that everything would be okay soon. Sometimes I wonder if human adaptability isn't actually one of the scariest aspects of our nature. It can allow us to get used to the most pathological situations. We find a syllogism to justify it all and just go on about our business.

I held a meeting to review conference logistics with Nancy, Gordy, and Claudia Caldwell from Meeting Planners (via speakerphone). We discussed the agenda, speaking times, all the minutiae involved with pulling off an event of this size. I ended the call by asking Nancy to fax a working agenda to Claudia, and I had all agree to meet the Sunday morning before the conference in the conference hall of the Westin Peachtree Plaza hotel in Atlanta.

After the meeting everyone left for lunch. I had planned to leave for home, but I tried first to reach Paula. I wanted to tell her about the dream. Her line at work was busy. I was about to call there again, but Lloyd walked into my office. I tensed up, putting the phone back on the hook with an embarrassingly unsteady hand. He didn't seem to notice. He didn't seem to be aware of much of anything, but he said he needed to speak to me urgently and lightly closed the door behind him. I hadn't seen him since Haviland's staff meeting, where it had become clear that he had somehow been involved with the discovery of the fliers.

"You know," he said, nervously lighting a cigarette, "eighty percent of life is just maintenance. You feed yourself, shit, wash yourself, buy new shoes, put gas in the car. It's maintenance, man, mostly maintenance. I think that's the basic drive behind the need for alternative consciousness. We're just so fucking bored with the maintenance, ya know. And then people expect shit from you too."

This wasn't at all what I had anticipated. This was strange behavior even for Lloyd. Disassociated psychobabble wasn't his style. But then he didn't look like his old self either. His eyes were bloodshot and wide, his face had the pallor of a sun-bleached oyster shell.

"You came in here to share this insight with me," I said, thinking he would respond to humor—it had always worked in the past. "Thank you, Baghwan, thank you."

"Hey, I'm serious, Bill! You don't understand. You've got to take a look at chaos theory, nonlinear systems, the laws that govern disorder to know what I mean. Entropy, man—the summit of fuckupedness. I know you know, because I know your secret. You've been putting on a good show."

"What do you mean by that? You've been spying for Haviland, haven't you? Tell me! Tell me! You've been spying on me, haven't you? Haven't you?"

He gave a kind of indignant snort and then a chuckle. Before I could stop myself, moving as if under the direction of a clean unfettered impulse, I grabbed him by the neck and pinned him against the wall.

"Tell me now, tell me the truth!" I demanded. But he just laughed in my face.

"I told you you were paranoid," he said, with an almost silly slapstick intonation, waving his finger in my face. "But I know your secret, man. You knew I wanted it, and you've been getting it yourself all along." Then he smirked and started babbling again. "You see, order is really just a statistical illusion—all that Newtonian stuff. But chaos is like a kind of order so complex that it just can't be predicted or explained, at least not—"

"Well, I know your secret too," I said swiftly, releasing him as I did. "Let's talk about addictions. What do you say?"

He shook his head, and his eyes quivered and went wet. "Man, you should have come to the car show with me. That new XJS coupe is hot. You'd like that car." And he just walked out, muttering to himself.

I had to get out as fast as I could. I was no longer in the

place I had worked for the last fourteen years, or if I was, the landscape had changed so radically over the last few months that I was no longer sure whether anything was or what anything meant. I had to get out before I was trapped. And I began to believe then that I would actually be trapped inside if I didn't hurry. I began frantically to stuff papers into my briefcase, and when it didn't seem quite full I stuffed my jacket into it too, and then everything else on my desk until after a while I wasn't even aware of what I was doing, just whirling around, knocking things off shelves, kicking over chairs. And then I stopped in the middle of the room, writhing and trembling like a believer touched by the spirit. I may have been crying or gibbering incoherently, I'm not sure. I remember running from the office out to the parking lot.

I was scrambling into my car when Carl approached me from out of nowhere. Seeing him was almost too much to take. He was smoking a cigarette and I saw there was nothing welcoming in his expression.

"You just couldn't make it to the meeting last night, could you?" he said.

"What meet—oh! Oh, I had a doctor's appointment. Look, I'm in a hurry."

"I was hoping you would be there. I told everyone you would be."

"What do you want me to say? I told you, I had a doctor's appointment."

"Fuck the goddamned doctor, Billy! You could have been there if you had wanted to—if Haviland had asked you!" I closed the door and started the engine.

"Where are you going? We've got the petition started! And it's going right to Haviland too. We want him to void the first union contract as unfair and then enter into negotiations with us as an independent union for a new contract."

I began to laugh; I couldn't help it. It just started coming out of me, convulsing forth, like I was throwing up. "Carl, you know what you're asking for isn't going to happen. Haviland isn't going to void a signed union contract that took months to negotiate. I don't even think he could legally do it if he wanted to. Don't you understand that? How could you have worked here as long as you have and not understand something that basic?"

He just stood there staring at me, wide-eyed, not knowing how to proceed. I had stopped the spasmodic laughter but I could feel myself beginning to tremble again, just mild shaking at first but growing stronger. I had to get away.

"We're going to fight, Billy. We're fighting for everything. How else will we get taken seriously? The hardest thing for a black man to be in America is taken seriously. You could have come to the meeting to moderate the situation, to bring some new ideas out. What you know about how things are done could have been goo—"

"I want to be left alone! Don't you understand? I don't want this! I don't want it! I don't want it!" I kept screaming it out as I drove away, not caring if everyone in the plant saw me—perhaps because I wanted them to know too.

I spent that night in the TV room drinking the fifth of Wild Turkey I'd bought at Alonzo's on the way home. All I really remember of the evening is thinking about the dream and the feeling of waiting to remember and the two merging in my mind like one thing.

In the morning Paula and I had a violent argument about what living with me had become. We didn't talk to each other for the rest of the day. But by evening I went to her and told her how some people at work were out to get me.

"I'm going to straighten things out in Atlanta," I remember saying to her. I told her about everything—except the attacks I'd had or anything else that sounded too insane. If she had wondered about my sanity before then, I'm sure after I finished explaining things to her she had no doubt at all but that I was losing my mind.

But she kept her cool, helping me to pack my bags, trying to play along as best she could, telling me at one point that she thought my decisions not to sign the petition or go to the meeting had been good ones. Then agreeing with me that Lloyd was probably a spy and that the best thing for me to do was go to Haviland first and tell him everything I knew. Then she asked if I couldn't do that over the phone, if it was really necessary for me to go to Atlanta. When I insisted she backed off, making me promise instead that I would get some rest, maybe drive down and see her father when I got back. It all sounded fine.

I remember how she clung to me that evening, as we lay in bed as if I were all that prevented her falling from some great height. Or was it I who clung to her? Somewhere in the middle of the night I felt it again, the waiting to remember, the question advancing—almost, almost. It wouldn't be long now.

sixteen

There is a lie I've allowed us both to believe for the last nineteen years and it's time now to be done with it. I've been hiding behind it for so long I've stopped remembering why. Or was it that I wouldn't let myself remember? I think I've always known, really, that fear was a partial culprit. Yes, I knew that acknowledging the truth would force me to confront the injury I did us both, and that I feared. It would have forced me to ask myself why, and in doing so I'd be asking that why to damnation because while there has always been my fear, dazzling and zealous, there has also been an anger I didn't want to contend with. I've been angry at you for nineteen years now, Paul.

I guess you know by now that it's the day at the creek I'm getting at. Do you remember it as clearly as I? Do you remember deciding to go fishing for white perch just once more for old times' sake? We brought along that beat-up umbrella net of yours so we could catch some grass shrimp for bait. And once we did, we sat there for a half hour without even taking a nibble from a perch. I don't think either of us cared though. We weren't really there to catch fish, but to try to come to terms with the fact that in another few weeks we would be leaving for college, me up to Maryland and you way out to Stanford. Perhaps it was by reason of all the discomfort and awkwardness that I declared, anyway, that the fish wouldn't bite until the tide changed. That's when you suggested a swim.

The water was cool because the nights that August had been unseasonably chilly. We waded out anyway, until the bottom got muddy. Then you started doing dives the way we used to, pretending to be Johnny Weissmuller going after a crocodile. You came up right beside me that last time, just standing there, watching me laugh.

"Man," I said, "you know, we've got to come back here next summer."

Then you asked a question. You said:

"Billy...you ever wonder what it would be like to hug a man?" You didn't bother to couch it in a joke or even to distance yourself from the question with your usual detached matter-of-factness.

I had stopped laughing. "You mean like a man hugs a woman? No! Hell no!" I would have let it drop right there, Paul. I would have ascribed it to your quirkiness, just like I had the magazine, just like I had (and I've never told you this) the comment Crystal made the day after she had spent that afternoon with you in her mother's bed. She told Nisey, "He didn't even act like he appreciate it." I knew what she meant. It was lack of interest, wasn't it? I'm pretty sure of that now. Even though I suspected it then, I would have let it all drop, Paul. I didn't have to know, and you knew that. But I could see in your face that you were determined to say it, despite everything. You said, "Well I've thought sometimes...what it would be like to hold...to hold you. I've wanted to hold you." Before today I was never really sure

168

why I did what I did next. I grabbed you by the neck and wrestled you into the water. And then I backed away, calling you a faggot, "a goddamned punk!" I screamed. I'll always remember your face then, wrenched and frightened. It was the last I saw of you that summer or since. I'm sure my grandmother noticed (and may have, after a fashion, even rejoiced over) your absence, although she never said a word. But after you sent those letters around, I think she put things together for herself.

Sometimes here in the evenings when there is only the shadow on the wall outside my window, I can still see you standing there in the creek and I know then that everything I did, or have said or not said to you since, was out of anger. I was mad that you told me. I felt as if you had left me with no choice but to repudiate you. And the lie, Paul, was that all of the outrage and indignation and disgust I heaped on you was just a cover for the anger, because I'd known about you all along. Why wasn't loving you like a brother enough? Didn't you know that telling me would mean our friendship would have to end?

I read that nowadays such friendships are more common. I guess the world has moved on since we built our walls. Although I don't think I'll ever completely understand about ... how you are. And I'm not absolving you totally either. How much could you really have expected me to accept in those days? But lying here, I've thought for the first time about your confusion, about what things must have been like for you back then. If I could only undo it all somehow, all the years I've thought to contact you and did nothing, all the wondering with regret. God I'm sorry for it all. It's almost as if not having your friendship eliminated anything I was. What's a life without a past to connect it to?

I look back over what I've lived and there is so much untended, so much I've winnowed out for fear, and anger, and simplicity's sake.

I know I've treated Paula badly this last month. What I would like to do this very minute is to hold her here close to me as tight as I could. Love and friendship are really all that makes it bearable, aren't they? I'm glad Paula's making visits here again. I mentioned that to Donna today and she just smiled and smiled.

seventeen

On the Sunday morning I was to leave for Atlanta I got up early and put my things in the car. After a good-bye kiss Paula's last words to me were: "Call me when you get to the hotel."

At the airport, I let the skycap take my bags from the car. The flight from Baltimore to Atlanta was an hour and forty-five minutes. Although this was weekend travel, I was wearing my best suit. A hide-colored double-breasted Armani, which I wore with a lavender shirt and an Ungaro tie of deep purple and dark honey brown. It was my travel suit, the perfect ensemble, businesslike but just enough verve to be distinctively tasteful. Each piece got noticed—the suit, the tie, the milk-chocolate-colored belt, right down to the Mauri loafers.

I always wore a suit when I traveled south. Call it paranoia, but I didn't want to be confused with the local folk. In a suit I imagined myself a thing of mystery and wonder—a sartorially resplendent quirk to the cabbies, gas-station attendants, hotel receptionists, the traveling southern housewives who always seemed to be seated beside me on planes. Judging from the way I'm stared at and questioned, I've concluded that in the Deep South a black man in a suit from someplace else is something to approach with curiosity. I base this observation on a scientific comparison. More than once I've traveled south in casual clothing and been treated indifferently, rudely, or even suspiciously by hotel clerks, convenience-store managers, waiters. So I started traveling in a suit.

The plane wasn't even half-full. I had an entire row of seats to myself. I passed the flight time eavesdropping on the conversation in the row behind me. Two men were discussing a class they were both traveling to attend. It didn't click until we'd landed and were leaving the plane that they had been talking about the same class Lloyd had described to me. Managerial Tactics. I confirmed this when, exiting the jetway, I spotted a short stocky man with cropped reddish blond hair, wearing a fatigue-style jacket and a pair of acid-washed jeans. In his hands was a large sign that read Bascome Conference Center.

I got a cab to the hotel. Once in my room and unpacked, I made my safe-arrival call to Paula. It was raining in Baltimore, thirty-five degrees, and she missed me. She also told me that she had called her father and that he would be visiting with us the week I returned. I said a long good-bye and then left for the meeting hall and my rendezvous.

I found Nancy and Claudia Caldwell sitting together near the stage. Claudia saw me come in.

"My, my, look who showed up," she said. Nancy turned to greet me. "We were just talking about you," Claudia continued as I came closer.

"Makes sense," I said. "My ears are burning."

"It was really complimentary," Nancy said. "Claudia was just telling me how well you dressed."

"Well thank you, Claudia. I guess we get charged extra for compliments."

"No, no," she laughed. "I've already built them into the price. No, I really like what you do with color. A lot of men seem to be afraid of color."

"What time did you two get in?" I asked.

"I got in early this morning," Nancy said, "but Claudia's been here since yesterday."

Gradually we began to discuss the details of the meeting. It took about an hour. Gordy never showed up, but Claudia seemed to have everything running smoothly. I made my exit by saying I had calls to make.

"I guess we'll see you this evening," Claudia said.

Walking back through the lobby I spotted two of our salesmen checking into the hotel. It was Tom Gorman and Alan Lester from the San Jose office. Alan was the hottest salesman in the company. Silicon Valley was a good territory to have, but Alan was a tenacious worker. He also had a well-deserved reputation for heavy drinking and rowdiness. I once saw him flamenco on a tabletop in a hospitality suite. I stopped to chat once they saw me. It was the usual glad-to-see-you-how-the-hell-are-you exchange. You shake hands, promise to have a drink together before the conference ends, and then you walk away.

Back in my room, I found I was unable to sleep. I drank a glass of water, turned the TV on and off. I peered out my window to see what I could of Atlanta's skyline. Finally, I stripped to my shorts and stretched out on the bed. I tried to force myself asleep, closing my eyes and lying as still as possible. But sleep never came, and when I finally opened my eyes I saw that the message light on the phone was flashing. How long had I missed it?

When I called the desk, the operator told me I had an

urgent call from Mr. Haviland. What was he doing in Atlanta already? I called his room and got no answer. I left a message with the operator. I dropped back on the bed. The anxiety was welling up inside of me again. I knew it had never really gone away. I cursed Carl under my breath. I cursed myself for not knowing what I would say to Haviland.

The phone rang about two. It was Haviland; he asked if I could come up to his suite for a meeting. He didn't sound particularly urgent, in fact he didn't sound urgent at all. But that didn't mean anything and I wasted no time getting dressed and taking the elevator to his floor. There was a Muzak version of "Hot Fun in the Summertime" filtering through the sound system. It seemed to mock me, trivializing some memory dear to me. Then behind the music I began to hear other things. First something very much like a pause, as if the music had rested on a few beats. Then her voice became clear, just above a whisper. *Don't mess up now. Don't mess up now.* She kept repeating it, from every inch of the elevator in all directions at once. *Don't mess up now.* It was making my head throb. Everything went out of control then and I can't say with confidence exactly what happened. All I know is this: the bell rang at the fifteenth floor, I heard music, and then I found myself crouched in the corner of the elevator. I don't know how many times, if any, the car had stopped between the sixth and fifteenth floors. I don't know who might have gotten on and off the car. In my bewilderment, I let the elevator door close. It stopped again at the seventeenth floor, where I got off and took the stairway down to Haviland's room.

What can I tell you, Paul? I was scared. There is no feeling I can think of more frightening than losing control of yourself and being unable to stop it. It's like choking, like getting water in your lungs and not being able to catch your breath. You can't keep from panicking.

When he opened the door, Haviland asked me if I was okay. He told me I looked peaked and I told him the same lie I'd told his secretary about having a headache.

"Hell, don't get sick now," he said as he closed the door behind me. "This is the hour before dawn right here."

He took a seat in front of the window, pulling the chair around so it faced into the room. When he sat, he was framed and shrouded by the profuse incoming light. Whether he had done this purposely, for dramatic effect, I don't know. But I had to squint to look at him.

"So sit down why don't you," he said. "Looking up at you hurts my neck." I took a seat. "So what do you have for me?" he said.

I stumbled with my delivery a little but I managed to get a question out. It was a sloppy gambit to forestall the inevitable. I knew I'd have to tell him something sooner or later. Instead I asked him why he was so concerned about the fliers. But John Haviland never misses a beat. I'm sure he knew why I'd asked the question, yet he ignored the obvious and legitimized the query with an eager answer. He was strangely relaxed about it all; in fact, he answered me with a story.

"My first job out of graduate school," he began, "was in the metal-etching facility of Rosette SemiConductor. Small company, they went under in seventy-nine. But when I was there in the sixties they were doing some really pioneering work in core logic designs. Anyway, one evening one of the local TV stations did a report on toxins in the workplace. You hear about that all the time now, but back then it was a really shocking report. The next day at work one of our secretaries, who was pregnant, got sick. Man, by lunch it was all over the building. The next day another pregnant woman got sick. One day that week every pregnant woman at the company was out sick. Not that there were a lot of pregnant women, but when they're all out at once people start to notice. Finally a bunch of secretaries refused to come into the building until it was checked out. Someone had suggested that there was contamination in the air-conditioning system. We didn't want all this to get out on the street, so we had some people come in and check out the AC system. It was fine. It had always been fine. It was group hysteria. If someone had pointed out at the time that the only people getting sick were women, the headlines would have been something like 'Sexist Rosette Officials Mini-mize Health Risks.' It would have been a disaster. It almost was."

I guess he saw the befuddlement in my face. What did any of this have to do with my question?

"I guess you're wondering what I'm getting at." He smiled. "The point I'm trying to make is..." He paused here contemplatively. Again, a dramatic effect? "I guess I just have a hard time believing that every black person in the shop is dissatisfied to the point of striking. I think it's like what happened at Rosette. What do you think?"

I could almost hear the systolic rhythm of blood engorging my arteries. It was as if all external sound had been sucked out of the room. There was nothing to say. The silence that had fallen between us seemed to be widening by leagues each second. Haviland was watching me for a reaction, but his question had been rhetorical. He didn't give me a chance to answer.

"I've known you since you've been with this company. Have I ever not done good by you?" he asked. "I don't understand why you didn't come to me with what you knew. None of this is about anything but economics. We need the Mexico plant. The Japs don't have these kinds of labor problems to slow them down, you know that. This is not some civil-rights thing and I don't want it getting blown into one." He sat back, his gaze unflinching, like someone watching a fly on a countertop just before he swats it. I finally found my tongue.

"How did you find out?" I said.

"I'm not really sure what I've found out. Lloyd saw a flier on your desk one morning. He even saw Carl Rice put it there. I had him do some asking around."

I was cursing Carl in my mind. It wouldn't have done at that point to explain everything to Haviland, to tell him I wasn't even involved in any of this and that I'd planned to tell him everything I knew. I did mention the latter, which he didn't respond to. He got up from his seat and walked to the window.

"I'm going to be blunt with you, Bill. I don't want this thing turning into a major legal battle. Let's forget for a moment about answering to the National Labor Relations Board, all the bad publicity we'd generate about taking jobs out of the country and what that might do to our stock. Your average investor is not above retaliation, especially if someone they know has been laid off. I know that's unlikely, but we wouldn't want our stock boycotted because the investor community believes we have labor problems we can't manage. Besides all that, a major suit would cost us capital we need for that plant. I want to squelch this whole thing as quickly as possible, and I need you to do it. I need you on the inside. It's time to take off your social-worker's hat and put on your executive's hat. As far as I can see your responsibility is with the company, Bill. If there's something else at issue here tell me."

"No. No, there isn't. What has Lloyd found out?"

"Only that there's going to be a strike—and the only reason I know anything about it is just coincidence. That bothers me. I'm wondering what else I don't know about. You know the morning that the kid ran from me? Well, I just happened to see Lloyd in the hall. It was just small talk. I was telling him what I'd seen, and I happened to show him the flier, and he remembered seeing Carl put one on your desk that same morning. If it hadn't been for that I probably would have thrown the thing away and forgotten about it."

"Why didn't you just ask me about it?"

"And say what? I didn't know what was going on. Jesus, Bill, I gave you enough chances to tell me. I certainly didn't want to accuse you of anything. I brought it up in the staff meeting; I even had you come by afterward to talk to me in private. There aren't many people I would have done that for."

"What exactly did you find out from Lloyd?"

"Nothing really. Two days ago one of Len's floor managers overheard a couple of black machinists talking about a strike. He also found one of those fliers. So I've really just put things together. It's not too much of a stretch to see Carl Rice figured into all of this. Now, what don't I know?"

I told him everything—just as I had threatened Carl I would. I explained what the fliers meant; I talked in detail about the petition he would get next week; I told him what I knew of Carl's involvement. And as I talked a heaviness slowly enveloped me. It was pressing me downward and then it gave, releasing me. I was moving away from myself, out of myself. I heard myself talking, knew what I was saying, could feel myself thinking, but at the same time I was apart. Unable to affect what was happening but aware of it, observing it almost. Voices and sounds began to take on an elongated quality, ascending away from me.

"We need to have Dulaney involved in this. He's the one that should be playing arbitrator here," Haviland raged.

I heard myself telling him that Dulaney had no credibility with the black machinists. "He's not trusted or liked and some even think he's racist."

"Shit! We're going to have to get back there tomorrow! Damn! This whole thing is going critical. You should have come to me sooner, Bill. We've got to nip this petition in the bud. I'm going to have to call legal in New York. Be prepared to leave tomorrow morning. In fact, you take the first plane out. I'll meet you there. You need to talk to Carl and whoever else is leading the machinists; I'm sure you can go places that I, or George Yardly, can't. What the hell does he think he's doing? You find him when you get back, you tell him that I want to see him! He's gone too far this time. Meanwhile, I'm going to have Yardly talk to Dulaney and legal. I'll see you again this evening at the kickoff. We'll set things up then."

Back in my room I was oblivious to the passage of time. I packed my things and then spent the next two hours pacing the floor. Anxiety was rolling through me in waves. As much as I tried I couldn't stop thinking about the chaos that was certain to ensue when I got back to Baltimore. I lingered on the word "chaos," trying to remember what it was Lloyd had said about chaos two days before. It still didn't make any sense. I saw my career in suspension. Haviland hadn't pressed me about not coming forward sooner with what I knew, but he had mentioned it enough to let me know he was gravely disappointed. But he also needed me on the "inside," he had said. I wonder now if that had tempered what he'd said to me.

eighteen

You must understand that I had spent my entire career avoiding situations where my race would put me at odds with my race, or my employer. And to a degree I had achieved that. The result was, however, that I had no real credibility as a black person at Varitech. I was not known by them, I had not associated with them, I had never gone out of my way to cultivate an awareness of myself as a black person. And the whites seemed to appreciate that. I had avoided association with black professional groups (the kind white upper management gives supportive lip service to and most white employees despise and label racist) and black professionals who were considered sensitive. (You see, to be labeled "sensitive" is the kiss of death for blacks in corporate America.)

On more occasions than I want to recall, a colleague has said to me something like, "You know, Bill, you're not sensitive like a lot of blacks." And to prove it they would tell me jokes (in good spirit, of course) and make comments that would have sent Carl ballistic. I listened and smiled through it all, good team player that I was. And I didn't always disagree with what was said, although I still question the intolerance and lack of concern that usually under-lay what they said. "What can I do about it?" is the most rhetorical question in the world.

But had I just been deluding myself? What had I really achieved? Carl wanted me to sign the petition because I was a black executive and would give his cause a certain clout. Haviland wanted me as the intermediary between Carl and the machinists because my blackness could possibly assuage them into stepping down their demands. I washed up and took the elevator downstairs.

An elderly couple got in at the fourth floor. A stick-skinny old man and his thin smiling wife. They were very genial. They made some quick small talk about how nice Atlanta was. Then the woman asked me shyly if I was with the Hawks. I made some benign comment about how I wished I had the money those guys made. What else was there to say? They were such a nice couple. Would it have done to question why they didn't ask me instead what company I worked for? It wasn't even basketball season.

We all got off at the lobby level but instead of going to the meeting hall, I headed for the bar. It was almost deserted. I figured that everyone was at the conference. During my delirium upstairs I had missed most of John's opening speech. What would a few more minutes matter?

At the lobby bar I ordered three bourbons and drank all faster than was proper. After the third drink the barmaid looked at me askance and said demurely, in her juicy Georgia drawl, "Na you just cain't be in that much of a hurrey."

And she was right; I wasn't. I ordered one last drink. After that I made my way to the hall.

Nancy, Gordy, and Claudia were all standing along the wall at the back of the room, listening attentively to the closing words of Haviland's speech. Nancy saw me approaching and motioned me over to her.

"We didn't think you were going to make it," she whispered.

"Conference call with Baltimore, couldn't be avoided. How's everything going so far?" I think they smelled the alcohol on my breath. They were all looking at me with this strained conscientiousness, the way people do when they want to avoid acknowledging the obvious. It was the same seasoned face of restive politeness given to disabled people in public places.

"Everyone's very impressed so far," Gordy said. "I've been listening to people."

"You know, John Haviland really is a pretty good speaker," Claudia commented casually. "A lot of CEO types aren't."

I nodded and turned my attention to the front of the room. I hadn't helped John prepare this particular speech and as a result I had no idea what he was talking about. I tried to stand against the wall and look as if I were listening attentively. But when a long enthusiastic round of applause began, it was a few moments before I realized that John had finished speaking. I only joined in the clapping near the end. Gordy took the opportunity to explain to me why he had missed the meeting earlier that day. I told him not to worry about it.

People were beginning to move toward the exits now. The banquet would be starting soon. I realized that as near the door as I was, my chances of getting stopped by someone wanting to chat were greater than I cared for at the moment. I was just beginning to feel the slow burning torpor of the bourbon. I wasn't a frenetic drunk, or a philosophical drunk. I drank for the depressant quality of the alcohol. I didn't want condolence, camaraderie, or conversation. I only wanted the opportunity to drink alone. I wanted to say nothing more cogent to anyone than Yes, that's right, another bourbon and water please; no ice.

But it was already too late for that. Most who passed just nodded and said a bright hello. But then Mark Dornberger from the Chicago office spotted me as he was rounding the last row of seats along the center aisle. Mercifully (Mark is a real talker) he only had a chance to shake my hand and say hello, because Charlie St. Claire from the Cleveland office came over, said hello to me, and then placed his hand heartily on Mark's shoulder and said something to him that sounded like "Here's raking the border!"

Whatever it was it must have been something big because Mark immediately excused himself, promising to talk to me later as he rushed off with Charlie.

I moved away from the door and went along the far aisle toward the stage. Haviland was leaning over the lectern speaking to Len. The small crowd that had gathered around them was dispersing. Lloyd and Nancy were standing nearby, having a conversation of their own. It was strange; as I came closer the light suddenly seemed unusually bright. Sounds seemed to be clearer, more discrete. It was as if all my senses had been gathered up in preparation. But for what?

And then it became clear. They all turned in unison to watch me approach—Haviland, Len, Lloyd, and Nancy, all of them, all at once. I shuddered at first; my eyes may have widened, because I knew unquestionably that I had been given a sign, a message in some new, frighteningly subtle medium.

My first impulse was to stop dead, as if their collective stares constituted a moving wall of daggers. But I continued, knowing that to acknowledge the message would somehow corrupt it. I wasn't sure what it meant, but I was certain it meant something. (I've learned since that psychologists refer to these episodes as events of reference.)

Haviland called me over and together with Len we discussed a quick agenda for tomorrow. I could hear Len whispering in his mind, saying over and over again how he knew I had been lying all along. *Trusting them is a mistake*, he was thinking to me. John spoke in his usual brisk to-the-point manner. I was to arrive first at the plant. I was to talk to Carl, get him to back off the petition, and if possible get the machinists to back off as well. Haviland wanted details about their grievances; he wanted me to find out where we could apply leverage. Most of all, and he was emphatic about this, he didn't want that petition to see the light of day. I was to give him a report at noon in a meeting that would also include Len, George Yardly, Jack Dulaney, and possibly one of the lawyers from New York. George, Haviland told me, was at that very moment briefing Dulaney back in Baltimore on what was going on. Nothing would be done though until after I'd given a report to the group.

Len wondered if there was anything more he could do before tomorrow. Perhaps he could have one of the floor managers call a few of the black machinists at home, or maybe he could talk to Carl himself and "get to the bottom of this." Haviland made it clear that this was mine alone to do. He and Len rushed off soon after that but not before he told me that he expected results. I nodded; I may have even made some jaunty statement assuring my success. I knew then that the message I had received was a warning. They were telling me that I was being watched and so should not make any mistakes.

Lloyd and Nancy came up to me and asked something about a drink. I had forgotten that they were even standing nearby. Nancy repeated her question but I listened without looking her in the face. Instead I was watching Lloyd. He'd known about this all along; he'd played spy for Haviland and had said nothing to me about it. He was the one who had probably arranged for everyone to stare at me in collaboration. He was, after all, Haviland's messenger.

This is where the lights went out, Paul, the point at which my senses were so inundated with conflicting signals that even the simplest comment was too complex for me to absolutely understand. It was like a web I was trying to assemble thread by thread, comment by comment, word by word. A statement, any statement, could no longer stand alone, everything was now connected somehow. This is the subject's view of insanity.

"Bill, we're going to go out for a drink," Nancy said again. "Why don't you come on with us? Or are you going to the banquet?"

I was still watching Lloyd and now he was watching me, twitching under my stare.

"Yeah, Bill, why don't you come along? Your job's done for the evening. I know a place just a few blocks away from here." He was trying to act in control but I could see his discomfort. He really didn't want me along, any more than I wanted drinking partners. But my suspicion was nudging me onward. I was beginning to believe that Lloyd had other messages for me; I saw an abstruse innuendo in his offer.

"What the hell are you staring at me for? Are you going or aren't you?" he said.

He was on to me. I would have to become more discreet.

"I didn't realize I was staring at you. Don't get paranoid," I said, smiling. "Let's go." I didn't stop to consider if I'd be missed or not.

We left the hotel to find Lloyd's drinking spot. I don't remember the name of the place. It was about a block from the hotel, not very crowded. The usual middle-aged regulars drinking alone at the bar, invariably engaging the bartender in the sort of mindless palaver that seems to sustain the distraught. And then of course there was the almost obligatory splattering of young urban professionals—the yuppies, poised and dandyish in their yellow bow ties, silk suspenders, their tortoiseshell specs and other buttoned-downed, French-cuffed, crisp-pleated, spit-polished declarations of station. They sat at their tables in grade-school style, boy-girl, boy-girl, engaged in what appeared to be the most anxious of conversations, never completely unaware, I think, that they were being watched.

The television above the bar was showing the local evening news, and there was music playing. I never saw the jukebox, but there was a Ray Charles song I didn't recognize coming from somewhere in that room. This bar was turning out to be a relaxing place, and I felt the tension and suspense slowly begin to abate.

Our waitress was less than prompt. We'd taken a seat at the back of the room, just past the remains of a ravaged snack table. When we were finally able to order, I had my usual bourbon and water, Lloyd a vodka and tonic, and Nancy wanted a screwdriver. For some reason Lloyd doubled over in laughter at that. Nancy and I looked at each other. Neither of us saw the humor in ordering a screwdriver. For some reason the laughter seemed directed at me.

"What are you laughing at?" Nancy said to Lloyd. "What's so funny about a screwdriver?"

"A screwdriver! A screwdriver, huh?" He could hardly speak for laughing. "Bartender," he said mockingly, "another screwdriver please." He was almost hysterical. "Another fucking screwdriver please!" He was laughing uncontrollably now. It didn't seem to bother him that neither Nancy nor I knew what he was laughing at.

"I still don't see what's so funny," Nancy said. She was beginning to laugh herself. "It's just a drink for Chrissake."

"Well, yeah," he said, "but you see, it's a screwdriver." He broke up all over again. "A fucking screwdriver in the Reagan eighties." He started to cough, he was laughing so hard.

They were both laughing so feverishly that they hardly seemed to notice my seriousness. I was growing increasingly paranoid. I thought the whole point of the laughter was to tell me something, to give me another message. Finally, Lloyd settled down enough to finish a complete sentence.

"Nancy, darling," he began, "no one over nineteen drinks screwdrivers. And if that isn't bad enough, it's a seventies drink. Screwdrivers went out with Jimmy and Billy and the whole disco-dancin' Carter era. That's not what the yuppified Reagan eighties are all about."

"So what is the drink for the eighties?" I asked, thinking there was some message here I was supposed to investigate.

"Ah, a man who sees the seriousness in this matter," Lloyd said. "Everyone knows that scotch is the drink of this decade. This is the decade of WASP reassertion! And by God we drink scotch!" He hadn't even had anything to drink. I couldn't tell if he was serious or just ranting. He began to laugh again and it confused me to the point of agitation. I wanted to grab him around the neck and tell him just to come out with what he wanted to say.

"Well, if what you say is true," Nancy said slyly, "why did you order a vodka and tonic? I guess you don't know as much as you think you do, sonny boy." She looked my way and began to laugh—more a jogging taunt than a laugh really. I eventually joined in too.

Without warning Lloyd's face bloomed into a crimson flush. He was enraged. His nostrils flared, his eyes seemed to bulge and moisten under great pressure, his breaths became short and predatory.

"What are you trying to say? Are you calling me a fool?" he said, throwing the word at her as if he were watching it ram into her face. "You two think you have me over a barrel, don't you? I know your secret too!"

In the midst of it all I realized that I was being tested. That was the message. It was a test of my courage. That's probably why they insisted that I come along with them in the first place. Haviland wanted to test my courage. He wanted to see if I could be trusted in a clutch situation.

"Lloyd—" I began firmly. But he cut me off before I could finish.

"No! Wait a minute!" he shouted, never taking his eyes off Nancy. "You think you got one over on me or something, don't you?" he said to her. And then to me: "No one talks that way to me! Don't think you can. You got nothing on me."

I realize now that he was in the midst of his own paranoid delusion. Our respective insecurities and insanities must have meshed nicely, because in a bizarre way I understood, or rather I thought I could connect everything he said.

"Just drop it!" I said.

"No! I want to know where you and your Polack bitch get off. You're not my fucking parents! Who the fuck do you think you're talking to! I know what you two have been doing. I know your little secret!"

I stood up. "That's enough," I said. He gave me a piercing nasty stare and for a quick moment I thought we were headed for violence. Instead, he exploded up from the table with such force that he almost knocked it over. He kicked his chair aside, still infected with that scalding crimson rage. We eyed each other warily. Then something seemed to come over him, something altogether unexpected. He suddently looked around as if he'd just come out of a trance, for an expression came over him of pure undiluted embarrassment. It was like witnessing something supernatural, as if we had just watched his possession and exorcism in the space of a half hour. He had managed to capture the attention of everyone in the bar. They all watched as he quietly walked out.

I think the upside of it all was that our waitress seemed to quicken herself with our drinks. She arrived at our table as Lloyd was walking out the door. She wanted to know if he was coming back.

"No," I told her, "he won't be back." It felt good to have passed the test. I could drink now with peace of mind in this strange new confidence.

But it was a while before Nancy could speak. She was shaking, near tears, letting out long nervous sighs with each sip of her drink.

"What the hell was his problem?" she said, a slight tremolo quality to her voice.

"I don't know. But I think I handled it okay, didn't you? You'll tell Haviland that, won't you?"

"Jesus," she sighed, not hearing or caring to acknowledge my last statement. "I think he's losing his mind. He's been acting strange all day, you know, staring at me and all."

Our waitress swung by at that moment and I ordered another round. This time Nancy wanted a Jack Daniel's and Coke. After two of those she began to regain her old self. We of course discussed Lloyd again. His erratic behavior of late had not gone unnoticed. That led to another discussion of his ambiguous position within the company. I didn't reveal any of the things Carl Rice had told me a few days earlier, but I began to wonder if Lloyd's present rickety demeanor wasn't an indication of a recurring problem. I'd never known a coke addict and so I didn't know what to expect.

After the third drink it became clear that Nancy had secrets to tell. I suppose not being a talkative drunk gave me the appearance of being a good nonjudgmental listener. Of course nothing could have been further from the truth. I wanted to be left alone, but my allegiance to my grandmother's notions of politeness was more faithful than I could imagine. I listened. We ordered more drinks.

Nancy began to talk about the office. She and Jack Daniel were going to share their unsolicited thoughts about our personnel. She started with Gordy. He was "basically a nice kid" who at times bordered on being a "punk." I had no comment. Dierdre was a "pushy JAP from Pikesville."

"Not that I have anything against Jews," she added. I think my silence was making her self-conscious. "But they do have ways about them that pluck your nerves."

What comment could I make? Even drunk I knew better than to discuss my staff with another member of my staff. But how to say this politely?

"I guess you think I'm being crude," Nancy said, taking another sip of her drink. "You're so refined. I've never met such a refined black man."

"Well, I'm one of three refined black men in the United States."

She laughed out loud at that, a loose slippery sort of

cackle that seemed to tumble out of her mouth. "You haven't said anything funny in a long time," she said. "You used to keep the office pretty lively. Something's been bothering you, hasn't it?"

I heard a message in that statement. I hadn't expected it but I heard it clearly. She was trying to tell me something. Quite automatically, I began to look for connections while answering her question.

"I guess I'm just suffering from the usual existential despair," I said.

"What?"

"Let's say I'm having a mild midlife crisis."

"Oh. I thought so. I watch you. You know that? I watch you all the time." She put her hand beside mine. "This summer I was almost as dark as you." She giggled. She was beginning to ramble. "Only mine fades away. Brown skin is so pretty. I used to go to this tanning salon in Glen Burnie, but I heard it could cause skin cancer. Do black people ever think it's strange that white people spend so much time trying to get brown?"

"We talk about it all the time. I think King even mentioned it in a speech once."

"Really? You're kidding," she cackled. "You're kidding! It's just that a lot of guys think brown skin and blond hair look really good—that California look, you know?"

Everything she said now was a message of some kind. I was desperately trying to make the right connections. It was like being a blind man locked in a room of brilliant white light. I knew it was there; I could feel it on my face, but I could not see it or see what it revealed about the room. I still had the chore of feeling around for answers.

"Have you ever really taken a good look at the women who have that California look?" I asked.

"Hey, I'm no lezzie," she said, spilling laughter. "I'm

sorry, I couldn't resist that one. What did you say—the women with that California look?"

"Yeah. Take a good look at them. Maybe it's a cultural thing, but most black people see that look as unattractive. Kind of cancerous looking."

"Really! I would have thought you'd think that brown skin looked good."

"It does, on brown people. But on white people, especially women, it makes them look old. I met this woman at the L.A. office last year. You know Guy Osborn, the sales GM out there? He introduces this woman to me as one of the young lions in the sales group. Later on after the meeting I started kidding Guy about trying to flatter that woman with the young-lion remark. When he told me she was thirty I almost dropped dead. She looked at least ten years older to me."

"Really! Come on, you're exaggerating."

"No I'm not. That woman had skin like an old catcher's mitt. And she was one of these lay-out-in-the-sun-all-day-go-to-the-tanning-salon types too."

"Well, I stay away from the salon now. Tell me something. I've wondered about this for a long time now. Why do black people call you Billy and white people call you Bill? Carl Rice will call up and ask for Billy and Len Townes or Mr. Haviland will ask for Bill."

I felt as if I had been struck by lightning, for within that question I saw the guiding pattern—the path along which everything had been leading. It was now clear what the message was—at least part of it. She had almost given it to me without subterfuge. She was asking me who I was. But why was she asking me this? What was the rest of the message? I could no longer contain my agitation.

"Who wants to know this?" I said. "Haviland? Len? Is that who wants to know?"

"What? I want to know. What are you talking about?"

When I saw that she wasn't going to drop her guard, I began to laugh the whole thing off as if it had all been a joke on my part.

"I guess I never noticed before that I had two names." I laughed. "My grandmother called me William."

"So, are you Bill Covington or Billy Covington? We'll forget about William since you aren't a little boy anymore," she said.

I could no longer pretend to find this all amusing. My laugh became labored and plainly counterfeit. "That's a hell of a question, I'll tell you." I chuckled apprehensively. Then I dropped the laugh completely. "Can I ask you something? Why is this necessary? Why do you need to do this? What is it that you want to know?"

"Bill! What's wrong with you? I don't want to know anything you don't want to tell me. Forget it. I didn't know it was a big deal. But I'm going to start calling you Billy. I like that better."

"No, I can answer the question. I can."

"What's with you? Forget it, okay? I didn't know I hit a nerve. I know how that is. I'm like that about my sister. You'd like her."

"What do you mean?"

"My sister. She's very pretty, very pretty." I was staring at her, deeply, intensely, trying in this way to court her gaze. I wanted to see if I could extract a thought from her mind, a thought so pure and laid-naked bare that it would be impossible to disguise. But she wasn't really paying much attention to me now. She was rambling on about her sister. In fact, we were both so wasted at this point I can't be absolutely sure if what I'm telling you is actually what happened. I didn't know what to make of what was going on. In my mind our conversation had collapsed into a fathomless abstraction. I wasn't sure I understood anything she said. It was like some oblique form of aphasia. The words made sense but there was always an inference of something more, another more pertinent level of meaning. It made me believe I didn't understand anything at all.

"Oh, I know I talk too much when I drink," she said. "It's just that you really would like my sister. She's so pretty."

I decided to ignore the real conversation and focus on the literal. Perhaps it would lead me somewhere, to the real message being encrypted.

"Stacy got all the attention. Guys were knocking themselves over to go out with her."

"I'm sure you had your share of attention," I said.

"You haven't seen Stacy. She's beautiful; she really is." She had grown sullen and reflective. "No," she said, almost to herself. "Stacy was the pretty one. I was the good one." She tried to laugh but it wasn't very convincing.

"Stop it. Stop being coy, Nancy. I can't see you not getting your share of male attention."

"Maybe now. Men didn't pay much attention to me when I was younger." Her voice seemed to belie an old pain she was now reliving. But I wasn't sure. She was telling me more; she was still giving me messages. "I was fat. I was fat when I was a young girl."

"That's hard to believe looking at you now."

"Well, it's true," she said, taking another sip of her drink. "I was almost forty pounds heavier."

Then the music was in my ear. It was the jukebox but it

sounded as if it were right beside me. I looked around the room. I still couldn't see it, but there was Brook Benton beginning his graceful baritone glide through "It's Just a Matter of Time." The entire bar seemed to affix itself securely in the same minor-key saturnine of the song. I wondered if the music had created the mood, or if the mood had necessitated the music. It was now close to midnight and the place had greatly thinned out. I'd lost count of how much we'd drunk. Even the yuppies had lost their zeal. Their textbook correct postures had dissolved into a catalog of listless slouches.

"And I hated men too," she said.

"You hated men? Why? I thought you wanted male attention."

"Oh right, what should I have been, grateful? Is that what you mean? When I was fat men wouldn't even look at me. I lose some weight and all of a sudden I'm wonderful. I start hearing pickup lines from guys all over the place. It hurts to think what you really are to most men. That your body is all they want from you; that all that hurt and loneliness was . . . I'm still the same person now that I was when I was fat! I thought they were phonies. I guess I still do. The few dates I've had don't generally hang around too long. My therapist said that I need to make an effort to have fun with men and not to think of myself through them. I'm trying; it's just that they, they fool you by walking upright! So, you going to give me some advice now?"

"Should I? I mean me? I'm in no position to give anyone advice. What could I tell you?"

"Oh, I didn't mean it like that," she said, looking glassy-eyed and penitent. "You're a nice man, you really are. I watch you around the office. You're very polite, a gentleman." She finished her drink.

"Well thank you," I said, looking at my watch. "Gentlemen don't keep ladies out too late. I think it's time to blow this place."

"Oh yeah," she said. "*Gone With the Wind* comes on tonight."

I paid the tab and we left. There was no moon that night, just low heavy clouds that smelled of rain. I was still wondering if everything she said hadn't been some secret metaphor. I kept playing it over in my head as we walked back to the hotel. I looked over at Nancy walking just a bit in front of me, still rambling on about her sister and how nice a guy I was. I began to wonder what she had meant about not liking men. Was she saying that by liking me I wasn't a man? Was this another test Haviland had set up to see how much of a man I was? Then there was the question of the names, Bill and Billy. I had never answered her question and I began to consider that it might somehow be linked to the statement she had made about not liking men. I continued to think about it.

Back in the hotel, we had to pass the lobby bar on our way to the elevators. Even before we got close I could hear the noise. With the evening's scheduled events now over, the bar was packed with Varitech people. It was like the final episode in some inane production on intoxication and corporate mayhem. There was laughter, smoking, drinking, people talking loudly to be heard over the din—which in an almost symbiotic way ensured that the room would remain loud. In the coiled symbolism of my thinking, it was all a grotesquery, like a detail from a Bosch painting—a garden of delights. At any other time I would have joined in the festivities. But I saw the revelry as a kind of visual anagram that held a message I could look at but couldn't quite see.

A few people who recognized me waved. Larry Gould

from Parsippany was laughing with his eyes closed and his head held back. Elliot Norton was biting his nails. Sue Petrona was talking to Rob Kane, unknowingly moving her hand up and down the neck of the beer bottle resting on the bar beside her. Darnell Stewart, the only black salesman in the organization, was writing something on a cocktail napkin.

We walked directly past Tom Gorman, who didn't even notice us as he leered across the table at Gabriella "Gabby" Alfanador, the newest sales rep in the New Jersey office. He was trying to get her to say the word "simpático."

"Come on," he said. "Say it, I can't roll R's."

"There is no *R* in it," she replied.

"In what?"

"In the word." She smiled knowingly.

"What word?"

"The word you keep trying to get me to say! Will you stop it, Tom! I'll get up and leave if you keep on."

"Come on, just say it, once. Come on; simpático. Simpático. Come on, say it just for me."

I saw Len at the far end of the bar talking to none other than the much-acclaimed Carol Zaks. In an old-boy company like Varitech, Carol was something of a celebrity. Not only was she one of the few women in sales, she had, two days before, been promoted to regional director. The entire Great Lakes area was hers and she was rumored to be heading for even greater things at corporate. This fact was explanation enough of Len's interest in her (let's call it preemptive butt kissing on his part). But at the time, all I could think was that he and Carol were talking about me. They both looked up at me as I passed and then seemed to quickly avert their eyes.

Nancy was pretty quiet until we got into the elevator.

"I've never seen some of these people drunk," she said, giggling. "I wish I had a Polaroid."

I pushed the button for the sixth floor. "What floor for you?" I said.

She told me she was on six also. Then she asked if I thought anyone had seen us walking by.

"I'm sure someone did," I said, believing that she had actually been referring to Carol Zaks and Len.

"I hope it doesn't start a rumor. That's all I need is for someone to say, 'I think I saw Nancy Maruski with a man at the sales meeting.'"

I took that as another piercing remark questioning my maleness. She was saying that people wouldn't know if I was a man or not. Haviland still wanted proof. I decided to do the most expedient thing. As the elevator moved upward, I reached out for her and pulled her close. I kissed her with a drunk's sloppy precision. Her embrace was one of only momentary surprise. There was soon nothing at all tentative in her response. She held on tight and stroked her thin hard lips against mine.

Her room was only three doors down from mine. We embraced again when I shut the door, taking greater tactual liberties this time, allowing ourselves that spurious intimacy of casual lovers. In short order we fell onto the bed, our bodies churning against each other like tadpoles in a shallow pool. Some part of me was taking wild satisfaction in knowing that I would finally be giving Haviland the proof he wanted. But another part of my conscious mind was beginning to present itself. It was talking through the haze of bourbon, through the corkscrew logic that, more and more, had come to characterize my thinking. There was an objective truth to my actions that I had overlooked.

Nancy excused herself, telling me she would be right

back. Left alone, I could hear it clearly—not a voice, but a real unmistakable thought. I rendered me weak and dispirited. (Energy decreases as entropy increases; isn't that a law?) I started to see things in a native state. I was a married man with a subtext of crises. I was in my secretary's hotel room, lying on her bed, waiting for her to emerge from the bathroom, in all likelihood naked from tit to toe. What was I doing? Aside from threatening adultery, I knew I couldn't achieve an erection. Panic suddenly heated my veins with an inductive ferocity. And when Nancy did reenter the room wearing only her earrings and shoes, I thought seriously about running out. But she bashfully asked me if I intended to keep my tie on, and I began to remove my clothes. They in fact came off quickly. I gave in to the desire. I pushed aside guilt, warmth, deference, the actualities of the occasion. Then, at the very moment I touched her thigh, a vision came to me. I tried in vain to subdue it, but it would not be vanquished. Even when I closed my eyes, I could still see myself using her in the most vulgar way, as a vessel for my own humiliation.

Understand that this was not the simple dumb niggerish lust of a morally stranded businessman. I was at once hellbent on rising to the imagined challenge from Haviland and at the same time well aware of the consequent disaster that had been augured in my own flesh. By the time Nancy went supine on the sheets before me, I was desperate. I climbed between her legs knowing full well that I could only go through the motions of seduction. When it became clear to her that I wasn't getting hard, she motioned me to kneel back. She said something—I'm not absolutely sure what—and then put her mouth around me. I remember nudging her to her back again. Right after that she began to transform herself.

She receded slightly into the sheets and then slowly emerged as white and brittle as a tooth, like a dream image that exists as a collective embodiment of some menacing rumination scarcely recognizable to the sentient mind. Gazing up at me with a leering smile, she parted her legs back wide, inviting me in. But I couldn't enter. She looked up, beckoning me still, but telling me with her refractory smirk that she knew I would never get past the threshold. I was trying to get hard, squeezing and stroking myself violently, muttering things I still don't recall. I don't know how much time passed; the very awareness of time seemed to shrivel from my consciousness.

I suddenly found myself past the point of exhaustion, speckled with sweat, kneeling between her thighs with my cock in my hand. She was only Nancy Maruski and I became instantly sober in my self-disgust. She pushed me aside and rushed off into the bathroom. I closed my eyes and slipped from the bed to the carpeted floor, curling myself into a naked fleshy ball like the larva of some large black beetle alone in a temporary darkness. I could hear her calling from the bathroom. She wanted me to leave. But I already knew I had to go. I began to put on my clothes. She shouted out a second time for me to leave and when I didn't acknowledge her, she shouted again. Just then I felt the question, the awareness of it. I froze, waiting for it, thinking it was now time. But it wasn't yet and in that moment of realization, the waiting to remember was supplanted by a feeling that I'd misplaced something. I kept trying to remember what it was. I knew it wasn't in the hotel but I didn't remember where or what it was.

I opened the door and brushed past Lloyd, whose presence I didn't acknowledge.

"See," he said. "I told you I knew your secret too! You've been getting it all along. I can play the game too." And then shouting, as I moved farther down the hall: "You try to hurt me, I come get you. Remember that. Remember!"

Time began to break up again. There was a sense of thoughts scattering away. I was in the elevator going down and then I was in the rain walking on a street somewhere far from the hotel. Faces floated past me, disembodied. Some wore expressions of repugnance, others a mixture of sadness and fear. Most displayed a very practiced lack of interest that I recognized as a guise I myself must have often donned. My recollections after that are fragmentary. Someone, somewhere, offered me something to smoke from a homemade pipe. A man stuck his head out from a box and asked me a question. I spat blood into a fire burning in a trash barrel. I was searching for someone, two people actually. I couldn't remember when I'd recalled that but I knew I was looking for these people and I had to find them. Nancy had asked about them earlier. Their names were Bill Covington and Billy Covington.

Then the sun came up; a ball of wet tempera flame, brighter and more brilliant than I'd ever seen it. I found myself staring out from an alley that smelled of stale urine. My clothes were soaked to my skin and I was shivering uncontrollably. When I stood a stiff shooting pain ran through my side. I lifted my shirt and found that I was badly bruised. There was a crust around the bottom of my nose that I soon found to be dried blood. I staggered to the edge of the alley until the shivering and pain forced me down again. My first thought was to hail a cab. But looking around, I knew that cabs didn't come to this part of town. I was in some no-man's-land of dilapidated buildings and mean streets. But even if there had been a cab to hail, I couldn't have paid for it. My wallet was gone. Instinctively, I looked to my wrist; my Rolex was also gone.

I got up again, took five steps, and then collapsed on the steps of what I took to be an abandoned row house. The entire building was festering with decay. All of the windows on the bottom floor were boarded up; the painted surfaces were peeling in large nasty scabs. I wanted to get up but I couldn't stop shivering.

Suddenly, there was a rattling from the door and something flew out at me, landing on my head, covering my face. I scrambled to pull it off before I realized it was only a blanket. Threadbare and scratchy, it smelled of smoked meat. When I took it from my face I saw that there was a woman standing in the doorway before me. Three small children stood cautiously behind her, mirroring her moves like little shadows.

"You caint stay heah," she said, not in the least disparaging. "Theys ah shelta fo y'all people right down a heel." She pointed the way. I heard one of the children whisper, "Nanna, what's wrong wif heim?"

"He jist some ole crazy homeless man," I heard her say before the door closed.

As I was attempting to stand, a trash truck pulled up to the alley. There were two young black men riding on the back wearing matching faded blue jumpsuits and Louis Vuitton ball caps. When they jumped from the truck I yelled out to them. I asked them how far I was from the Westin Peachtree and they burst into laughter.

"I say you quite a ways," one of them laughed. Then the driver of the truck emerged. A weathered, dark man—dark in that regal blue-black pastel darkness of the abandoned sailor in the Winslow Homer painting. He was dressed in a style suggestively African. A brightly colored and intricately patterned jacket that seemed ill suited for his line of work. And he was wearing one of those little round brimless caps. Hip young black actors wore them in movies; black men and women in music videos wore them. Paula said they were popular with the kids at Morgan where she worked. She called them African hats. I knew no better and had adopted the parlance as well.

The driver studied the younger men, who were still snickering at me. He spat with a deprecatory flair.

"Man, y'all oughta be shot, laughin' at the brotha. He's been driven to it. You can look at 'im and see it. Hey, that's okay," he yelled to me. "We ain't none of us niggas."

The two other men folded up with laughter at that.

"Yeah, dat's right," one of them shouted, "you da king ah Einglan."

"Nah," the other man chimed in. "Look here, man, dat's Mista Rhett there. Rhett Butla. Frankly, I don't know where the mafuckin' hotel is." They both laughed.

The driver spoke again. "I wish y'all could see how pitiful you look," he said, shaking his head again. "We gotta stop helpin' the white man h'miliate us and start helpin' our own. Look, brotha," he shouted to me, "there's ah shelta right down the heel there. They ah take care ah you there."

"I don't want to go to a goddamned shelter!" I screamed, not aware of how the anger had been welling up inside me, not aware of how humiliated I was beginning to feel. "Look, I need to find the Westin Peachtree Plaza. I work for the Varitech Corporation and I have to get on a plane back to Baltimore today!" The two men in the jumpsuits laughed with a renewed vigor. They had finished emptying cans and were now just standing by the truck laughing.

"I guess he dist' ya shit, Mo," one of them sneered to the

driver. "Moe D. Mohamid," the man continued, "the black-ist brofa I know. I tell you what, Mo, whyaln't you jist take dat crazy nigga ta dat hotel and boaf ah y'all can walk in'nere—wif him all funky and fucked-up lookin' and you be beside'im wif ya Afrikin talk, ya Afrikin clothes, ya, ya, kufi hat, and you'ah fine out quick jist how much of a nigga you is. You an'nat crazy-assed mafuckin' bum!" he said, pointing to me and shouting for emphasis.

The other man, who had never stopped laughing, spoke up in agreement, saying, "Yep, yes indeed," as if he were testifying in church to the power of Jesus.

The driver stood stone faced, watching me. He looked down at the ground and I heard his breath released in tired expiration. I realized at that moment how I must have looked to them all. I had no way of proving who I was or much less what I did. It almost seemed funny to me in some lurid way. I pulled myself up from the steps, and staring at them all, I began to laugh. I drew the blanket around my shoulders and I continued to laugh, louder now. The men in the jumpsuits were no longer laughing and the driver of the truck was staring at me with an expression that bordered on frustration. I laughed until I was out of their sight, until I had passed the shelter. I laughed until my throat was swollen and dry. And then I just stopped. Right before me, framed between the edges of two other buildings, rising like a thick glimmering glass exclamation point above the city, was the hotel. It had seemed almost to come upon me. I had no idea how close I had been; no more than six blocks away it was. And then I found I couldn't go any farther. It wasn't fatigue, but something more. I sat down on the sidewalk against the wall of a building and pulled my knees tight to my chest.

I had at last reached the end of myself—a place rank

with the memories of deprecation, and pain. But hadn't my entire life been a pilgrimage to this place? It's where you end up when you divide yourself, and it's haunted by the ghost of that other, the invisible man I kept interred in the ivory shell. Who was he that we should not have stood together in such a long time? And suddenly the question gestating for so long, never far from my awareness, began to come to me at that moment. I waited now, feeling it, slowly, slowly.

Who are you? I whispered inside myself.

A voice came back, my voice and not my voice, talking through me.

I am William Billy Bill Covington, it began.

And a thought came to me so quickly, Paul—so quickly that I knew instantly, without saying or thinking, what the voice had told me. It said: They are who I had always been, no matter who I had assumed they were, no matter who I had thought they were not, no matter who they each dreamt I might have been. It didn't matter. Because we three are all one part of a larger body, this brooding fecund unconsumable blackness. A blackness that I now see will never be fully assimilated. It will always stand abject and separate even to the most well intended, if only on some discrete level of intuition or observance distilled in a nanosecond to a heedless reaction. It's the idea of this blackness that they see first, regardless. Blackness as the depreciated reciprocal of whatever whiteness has come to mean. This is who I am. I am inseparable from this blackness, its history, its weight, its obligations. Yes, obligations. Perhaps this is the real ghost that haunts that place I fear within myself.

All pilgrimages lead to choices we are obliged to make.

My grandmother whispered into my ear that it was time to leave. But I already knew that. She would be with me now to the end, telling me what she thought I needed to know. She wouldn't like what was going to happen, but it was like casting off a skin I'd outgrown—it was a requisite step for going on.

We stood up and began walking toward the hotel. At the registration desk we received startled and suspicious looks, a request for my Social Security number, and the assistance of Tom Gorman (who just happened by). He assured everyone that I was who I said I was. Only then did we get another key to the room.

I changed and showered, packed my bags—I had two hundred dollars in cash stowed away in one of them. We took a cab to the airport and then waited there for two hours to catch the next flight to Baltimore. We got into BWI at two o'clock. In her brief harsh whispers she reminded me of my mission, of Haviland's instructions. But I already knew what I had to do. She let me know she didn't like it, but I pushed her back.

■ ■ ■

The meeting in Haviland's office had already begun and I planned to be in attendance. But there were things to do first. I had to talk to Carl. We went to his office and found him at his desk, cigarette between his fingers, cup of coffee pressed to his lips, leafing through a book entitled *200 African Names*. He was all in black today—tie, slacks, and a charcoal Pronto-Umo cardigan with little amber flecks. He didn't seem at all surprised when he looked up and saw us coming through the door. He simply put the book down.

"Well, well. This is a surprise. What are you doing here? I thought you were in Atlanta writing me off."

"You know why we're here," I said.

"We? I know why I'm here. I'm waiting to take a petition to Haviland. I can't imagine why you're here."

"I think you know. Where is the petition, Carl?"

He dug into his pocket. "It's right here," he said, continuing to speak as he fumbled with a set of keys. "You know what they're trying to do is wrong. This operational seniority-plan shit is a scam, pure and simple! They make sure the white boys get promoted and trained on the new equipment first so that they always have more seniority than any of the brothers. And of course it's the brothers' jobs that get phased out or moved to Mexico."

When he opened his desk the petition was in the top drawer. For all of the scrambling and uncertainty and chaos it had set in motion, it was just a stack of paper. I suppose I had been expecting something more formal looking, something on parchment, written in blood. I motioned for him to hand it to me and when he did I signed it, page one, right at the top.

It took him a few seconds to register what I'd done. "Did you really sign it?" he said, looking at the page to make sure. He settled down a bit, staring at me as if he'd just watched me raise the dead. "What's this all about, Billy? What's this mean?"

"It means that we're going to a meeting," I said.

"What? A meeting; what meeting? What are you talking about?"

I'd never seen Carl this unsure. It struck me as funny and I laughed lightly. "You should hear yourself, Carl," I said. "I don't think I've heard you ask this many questions in all the time I've known you."

He gave me another tentative look, as if he couldn't decide what to say next. Then he asked, surrendering to the question, it seemed: "So, where are we going? What do you mean a meeting?"

"You wanted to see Haviland, so we're going to see Haviland. I can get you that, but you're on your own afterward. Come on, I've got other things to do today."

She took a place behind us whispering caution into my ear as Carl and I moved slowly along the hallway toward Haviland's office. She now knew what was going to happen and she kept warning me, reminding me of what I would be walking away from, asking me if I knew where I would go. I pushed it all aside for the moment. I knew for certain what I'd already lost and nothing seemed worth that.

As we went down the hall I explained to Carl as best I could what he would be in store for. He didn't have much in the way of comments. He just listened as I told him about the National Labor Relations Board and the channel this grievance should take if neither the union nor the company was willing to make some sort of deal. Finally, after I had told him all I possibly could, there was silence. We just walked. I had some loose ends, things I hadn't yet said.

"I've been thinking about your African name. I think you should keep Carl Rice." We turned the corner.

"That's not a surprise, Billy. You already told me that."

"I guess what I mean is that what you want doesn't seem recoverable to me. Isn't Carl Rice who you are now? Your name is you, for better or worse; it's what you've endured; it's what your parents and grandparents endured. It's yours. To change it would be like erasing everything, letting them off the hook. Put an American flag on your desk, Carl, it's more ours than anyone's. We should demand it, it's the only one we have really."

"Well, I've certainly never looked at it that way," he smirked after a reflective silence—which he again let grow between us. There was something more pressing on his mind. I knew what he really wanted to say. It could have only been one question.

"What made you sign it, Billy?" he said.

"What did I have to lose? There was no way I could have stopped anything—you, the petition, or even Haviland's demands. Oh, but I don't guess you know about that. Haviland wanted me to convince the machinists to drop the petition."

"I see. You told him no an—"

"I told him I would."

He seemed surprised by my admission. But he was still in a listening mode. He just shrugged and said, "So what happened? Why did you sign?"

"I asked myself a question and this was the only answer I could live with. It was a choice and it wasn't—I mean, it was decided already, like, like—"

"Hey, I understand. I knew eventually that you would do the right thing, that we would come together on this."

"I don't know if we'll ever come together, Carl. I'm not sure there's a way, I'm not even sure—"

"You know, Billy, you could find another job almost anywhere. You make it sound like it's over. You've got a lot of experience. You could—"

"Thanks, but it's not that easy. Who's going to be a reference for me here at Varitech? I've been working here most of my adult life. I'll have to account for it. After this, the word will get around, you know. It's an incestuous industry. You know, Carl, you should be worried about that yourself."

"Don't worry about me; I've got investments. You can't be out here working for them without something of your own to fall back on. Besides, I'm okay." We had come up to the door of Haviland's office. We lingered out there for a moment.

"I want you to know, Carl, that I don't consider any of this your fault. I did, but it's not you who's liable." He nodded and there was a brief calmness to his face.

"I want you to know something else too. All I'm doing for you is getting you in the door. And one thing more. Remember one thing. You have to make concessions; you have to give up something. That's the price of being in. They're going to be expecting that in there. There's no other way."

He raised his eyebrows in a question and started to move toward the door. "One day, Billy, you'll have to tell me what we have left to give up."

nineteen

The meeting was just short of a rout for Carl. He started in by suggesting that Len and Jack Dulaney were the initiators of a program to steer blacks into dead-end positions. But Haviland stopped him before he could get much further by asking how he had obtained his authority to represent the machinists. "I thought that's what we kept Yardly here for," Haviland said. When Carl couldn't give an answer that mattered, it was all over. What saved him, for the short term at least, was Haviland's lack of immediate options and my signature on the petition. When Haviland saw it, he ended the meeting. He said he wanted a "cooling-off period," but I knew he wanted an explanation. He wouldn't proceed until he had gathered in all the variables. In the meantime, George Yardly would be conferring with corporate legal in New York, Jack Dulaney would be meeting with union higher-ups, and Len would be covering his ass. Carl was asked to bring one of the machinists to the next meeting. Everyone would be more prepared next time.

After the room was clear Haviland and I remained seated at the table. I knew instinctively I was to stay; it was not something I had planned—there were no plans now, only the actions that conviction demands. She was there with us also, lamenting silently.

"Last night Lloyd had a talk with Nancy Maruski," he said. He hadn't bothered to close the door and he wasn't looking me in the face, but staring into the wall behind me. "She told him about the incident she'd had with you. Sexual harassment is a serious charge, Bill. If she wanted to go forward with making some sort of formal action, there wouldn't be much the company could do for you. And besides all that, I wouldn't want to see Paula have to go through it. I've always liked her." He looked me in the face. I had forgotten all about brushing past Lloyd at Nancy's door last night in Atlanta. "Are you losing your mind? I want this petition and all of this bullshit from Carl dropped! His ass is already history around here. I thought I had made it clear what your job was. People who don't do their jobs lose them, you know." His tone softened a bit. "Look, Bill, this isn't a civil-rights problem. I thought we'd discussed that in Atlanta. It's about doing business. Do you really believe Len Townes is a racist? Come on. He can be a little full of himself at times but I don't think that makes him a grand dragon either."

"He wouldn't have to be a grand dragon to be a racist."

"What?"

I was about to make another point but he interrupted.

"Look, Bill, I'm not going to debate Len's goodwill with you. Len Townes is not the issue. Neither of us has the time to waste on issues that don't matter. The point is, regardless of what you think about Len, you've managed to work with him without any problem for all these years. If Carl Rice wants to feel important he's going to have to do it somewhere else. And I'm going to see to that! Just remember what you've got at stake here; remember that the next time you put your name on something."

"There's nothing I can do, there never was."

"The first thing you can do is talk to some of those machinists. Tell them I sent you. Tell them I'll personally guarantee that the training selection process will be looked into. I think we can count on the union backing us for a change. They don't want this kind of press any more than we do. We can nip this thing if you can turn those machinists around. Consider Carl my problem. Now excuse me, I've got to call New York to answer for this mess. No petitions, no strikes, remember."

And as I was walking out the door he added, "Say hello to Paula for me."

I stood just outside the doorway and listened briefly. During his phone call, Haviland went on to plan a meeting. I heard him sketch out a contingency plan for dealing with the union. He discussed various scenarios of how the situation might escalate, of the legal positions the company could take. He really was a remarkable businessman. But he made no attempt to address the legitimacy of the complaint, no attempt to understand why or how things had come to the point of combustion. It was a business problem to him. Truth didn't matter, responsibility was risk, understanding was in the way. He just wanted the whole thing to disappear, preferably on his terms. The goal seemed to be to arrive at a position of mutual and agreed ignorance, like an out-of-court settlement where no complicity is admitted, no problem is acknowledged. In exchange for money and silence, everyone walks away like nothing was ever wrong.

And to be honest, I don't know why I should have expected anything different. That very visceral barricade of racial disparity, whether real or imagined by the offended or the offender, is a wall scarred with failed intentions. There is such a phalanx of emotion, history, quiet engendered discomfort, and outright hate that I don't know if those battlements can ever be breached.

We went to my office and phoned *The Sun*. There was a number you could call to report newsworthy happenings. I told of the goings-on at Varitech to some unnamed voice and then I left the building for what would be the last time. I knew I would never be back. I took nothing from my office because there was nothing there I needed. We drove home, without stopping by Alonzo's for a drink. She was being quiet now, but I could feel her sulking. I could feel it as a growing tightness about my body.

Paula was surprised to see me home so early. She was in the TV room watching "Jeopardy," halfheartedly doing a crossword puzzle.

"What happened?" she said. "I thought you were in Atlanta all week." Until she said that I'd almost forgotten that I had been there. It was like talking about someone else.

"There's been a change in plans," I said. "Actually, I just couldn't stand being away from you and I rushed home." I kissed her on the cheek. An almost unfamiliar look came over her face, it had been so long since I'd last seen it.

"It would be something if you really meant that," she said. Her pensiveness would begin to dissolve slowly during the course of the evening.

"Of course I really mean it." I suggested dinner somewhere downtown, perhaps the new Indian restaurant tucked unimposingly on the corner of Madison and Charles. She remembered hearing that the lamb was good there.

As luck had it, bad weather would force us to stay in that

night. We ended up eating in the dining room by candle-light, a steak dinner that I fixed. We finished the one bottle of Cabernet left in the wine rack and then I found the half bottle of Wild Turkey I kept stashed in the bottom drawer of the china closet. Paula mixed hers with a little bit of Diet Dr Pepper she had left in the refrigerator.

"You know wasting good bourbon like that is a sin," I teased.

"I don't see how you can drink this stuff straight," she said. Then she paused, looking at me as if she were trying to make a decision about something. "Please don't get drunk tonight, please. You get . . . "

"I'm fine, don't worry." I was watching her. Her eyes looked smoky behind the candlelight. "You know, I don't think you've aged a minute since we were married," I said.

She sipped a little more of her Dr Pepper and bourbon. Despite her request to me, she'd had a little too much to drink herself. As is wont to happen when she is mildly drunk, she developed a bad case of the clumsies. She soon began her particular ritual of penance. She dropped her silverware and apologized for it. She apologized for talking too much. She eventually apologized for apologizing.

"Will you please stop saying you're sorry for everything," I said. "Let's go upstairs; I've got a surprise for you."

"What's gotten into you today?" she gushed.

"You'll be asking yourself that in a few minutes."

"Oh, Billy, I wish we coul—," and she stopped herself, bringing her hands to her mouth in midsentence. I could tell she thought she'd ruined everything, but I reassured her.

"Feel," I said, taking her hand and placing it just below my belt.

"It's hard! Is that really you—I mean, I'm sorry."

"It's all me." I laughed. "Let's go." I took her hand and we ascended the stairs, just like a scene from an old Susan Hayward movie. We made love that night until alcohol and exhaustion caught up with us. I awoke to the sound of sleet spattering against the window. She was still sound asleep. I got up and found my robe and began to wander around the house. What a great old house. I took note of everything: the wood floors, the vaulted ceiling in the living room, the huge flagstone fireplace. I opened doors to feel their heaviness, I tapped the wood paneling on the living-room walls. I peeked outside at the Jag, slick and wet under the street-light. Damned if it didn't look like a big cat crouching, set to pounce.

What you gonna do now? She sounded different, farther away.

What you gonna do now?

I didn't have an answer, but she continued to ask.

"I don't know," I said.

I began to consider the question. What would I do? I had enough savings to keep us afloat for a while, but eventually I'd have to find a job—and then what? I saw us losing the house. I saw us losing everything. I thought about Haviland's veiled threat of bringing Nancy forward with her accusation. Maybe Paula wouldn't believe it.

"I don't know."

From the corner of my eye I saw something move across the floor. I dashed out to the dining room and saw a shadow slip past into the kitchen. When I looked out, the basement door was open. I went back upstairs and into my closet. From the breast pocket of an old suit I removed my gun. It had been my grandfather's pistol, a six-shot .32-caliber revolver that he kept in the nightstand beside his bed because for some strange reason she would not let him keep his shotgun in the room they slept in.

I padded downstairs, thinking again of the Jaguar. She was still asking me about my plans.

"I don't know, shhhhhh."

I couldn't decide whether to turn on the basement light from the top of the stairs or to rush down with the flashlight. I did both. I turned the light on and made a mad dash down the basement steps, and there I was at the bottom, waiting for me, still hearing her and still telling her, "I don't know, I don't know."

And then I didn't want to hear it anymore. I looked at myself up and down and then I couldn't stand to look any longer. I held the gun up and she laughed.

You might as well, you just another nigga now. It was her I wanted to get rid of. I didn't want to hear her anymore. And I agreed with myself. I put my hand over mine and squeezed and then I heard the snap and felt the sting. Like I told you, just like a white-faced hornet.

twenty

I found out from Donna what had happened at Varitech. There was a big write-up about it in *The Sun* a few months after I came here, but I was in no shape to read it then.

The company moved its operations to Mexico just as planned. But they offered a beefed-up severance package and set up a job-referral service to anyone displaced by the transition. There was no mention of anyone except George Yardly, who was quoted as saying, "Varitech believes that our people are our biggest asset."

I don't know what happened to Carl. No one from the company has written either here or to the house. I've been receiving my full salary since I've been here. That's something I know only Haviland could have arranged.

I think I've finally learned to walk again. Mastering a cane is not as easy as it might look. But I've got it down pat; everyone's surprised at my progress.

Paula's convinced she'll have a boy. I felt her stomach today as that baby kicked like it was in a race. Of course if she's right we'll name him Daniel and if we bring a daughter into this world we've agreed on Naomi, after Paula's mother.

I have a new project now. Forget the old one. Talking to you like this has shown me some new possibilities. What I have in mind may not turn out to be another way after all. I may even find myself back in this room again after it's all over. But the question begs an answer. I won't write to you about it now, but expect a letter from me in a few months. I'll only say that I realized that I have something I need to return, something you and I gave to each other a long time ago. It'll be a demanding project, but that's my own fault. I forgot for a while that it was unfinished and now I'm way overdue. There's a trick to it, you see. It involves travel and exotic places, and exploring ancient ruins others would just as soon leave alone. Does that sound like something you would be interested in?